What
Hitler
Knew

Zachary Shore   The Battle for Information in Nazi Foreign Policy

What
Hitler
Knew

OXFORD
UNIVERSITY PRESS

2003

OXFORD
UNIVERSITY PRESS

Oxford   New York

Auckland   Bangkok   Buenos Aires   Cape Town   Chennai
Dar es Salaam   Delhi   Hong Kong   Istanbul   Karachi   Kolkata
Kuala Lumpur   Madrid   Melbourne   Mexico City   Mumbai
Nairobi   São Paulo   Shanghai   Taipei   Tokyo   Toronto

Copyright ©2003 by Oxford University Press, Inc.

Published by Oxford University Press, Inc.
198 Madison Avenue, New York, New York 10016

www.oup.com

Oxford is a registered trademark of Oxford University Press

Library of Congress Cataloging-in-Publication Data

Shore, Zachary.
What Hitler knew : the battle for information in Nazi foreign policy / Zachary Shore.
    p. cm.
Includes bibliographical references and index.
ISBN 0-19-515459-2
    1. Hitler, Adolf, 1889–1945. 2. Germany—Foreign relations—1933–1945.
3. Nationalsozialistische Deutsche Arbeiter-Partei. 4. Germany—Politics and
government—1933–1945. 5. World politics—1933–1945. I. Title.

DD256.8 .S46 2003
943.086′092—dc21   2002074886

9 8 7 6 5 4 3 2 1

Printed in the United States of America
on acid-free paper.

In Memory of

Michael Aris

March 27, 1946

to March 27, 1999

Research Fellow,

St. Antony's College,

Oxford

and

Kenneth Jernigan

November 13, 1926

to October 12, 1998

Leader of the

National Federation

of the Blind

Acknowledgments

In writing this book, I drew upon the advice of numerous scholars in Great Britain, Germany, and the United States. While I am grateful to each of them, my greatest debt is to Prof. Emeritus Anthony J. Nicholls of St. Antony's College, Oxford. This book is in large part a result of his knowledgeable input and advice.

As I developed this manuscript, the following scholars either advised me along the way or read and critiqued parts of it in various stages: Lord Alan Bullock, Alon Confino, Lord Ralph Dahrendorf, Wilhelm Deist, Robert Evans, Shinju Fujihira, Michael Handel, Talbot Imlay, Robert O'Neill, Alistair Parker, Reinhard Rürup, Avi Shlaim, Harold Shukman, Jill Stephenson, Jonathan Wright, and Michael Zuckerman. President Richard von Weizsäcker a.D. kindly permitted me to view his father's official and private papers housed in the Bundesarchiv Koblenz. I am grateful for this access.

Several colleagues and friends deserve special mention for their tireless proofreading. Samuel Gregg of the Acton Institute and Elizabeth Miles of St. Antony's College consistently offered valuable comments and criticisms. I was blessed to find two principal readers, Maren Jacobs and Irene Ostertag, who came to share both my enthusiasm for this project and the excitement over our discoveries. My editor, Susan Ferber, helped smooth the manuscript's rough edges, while Dominic Hughes, Jany Keat, David Odo, Lynne Davidson, and Trudy Kuehner (the "bionic editor" at *Orbis*) assisted in the final revisions. One other individual has served as a steadfast supporter over many years. Prof. Stephen Schuker has continued to encourage me—often through the harshest of criticism—to work harder and to "get it right." His devotion to scholarship has inspired me.

I have also benefited from generous financial support from a variety of sources. The University of Oxford supplied me with funds for study and research, including the Scatcherd European Research grant and the Overseas Research Scheme Award. The University's Southern Trust Fund paid for the cost of my readers, without which I would not have been able to undertake this work. The Oxford Faculty of Modern History and the International Studies Centre both provided me with research grants. St. Antony's College provided financial support as well. The Royal Historical Society, the German Academic Exchange Service, and the Gore Family Memorial Trust Fund each contributed magnanimously to my research.

I was especially fortunate to have received assistance from every German archive I visited. The staffs at the Federal Archives in Koblenz and Berlin Lichterfelde were consistently friendly and helpful. Special mention must be made of Dr. Peter Grupp at the Foreign Ministry archives in Bonn, who was subjected to my incessant questions, yet always answered my queries with patience and precision.

Finally, this book could not have been possible without the generous financial and intellectual support from Harvard University's John M. Olin Institute for Strategic Studies and its outstanding fellows. The institute's directors, Samuel P. Huntington and Stephen P. Rosen, both took an interest in my work and contributed valuable suggestions for its improvement. And to Stanley Hoffmann, for his aid, support, and counsel, I am deeply thankful.

Above all, I have been blessed to have had the support and encouragement of my loving parents. Their moral support has meant more to me than I can express.

August 11, 2002   Z. S.

Contents

Abbreviations

ADAP   Akten zur deutschen Außenpolitik, 1918–1945

Aufz.   Aufzeichnung

BA K   Bundesarchiv Koblenz

BA BL   Bundesarchiv Berlin-Lichterfelde

DGFP   Documents on German Foreign Policy, 1918–1945

TMWC   Trial of the Major War Criminals Before the International Military Tribunal

PA   Politischesarchiv des Auswärtigen Amts, Bonn

VfZ   Vierteljahreshefte für Zeitgeschichte

**What
Hitler
Knew**

Introduction
The Darker World

Imagine yourself as one of Hitler's diplomats. From the very beginning of Hitler's rule in 1933, you find yourself serving a violent regime. Each day you read or hear about mass arrests, beatings, and murders. Communists, Socialists, trade unionists, Catholics, Jews, and others are being persecuted by your government. SA thugs in uniforms roam the streets in paramilitary bands, picking fights with those who fail to salute them, beating and sometimes slaying their victims.

You try to convince yourself that you are safe, that you are not an "undesirable." You do not belong to any of the targeted groups. But you are also not a Nazi Party member. And your colleagues at the ministry, all aristocratic, "old school" diplomats, are under increasing pressure from the newly formed state security services.

You can no longer speak freely on the telephone without fear that your line is tapped and your voice recorded. Conversations among colleagues and friends are charged with an undercurrent of tension. Your mail and telegrams are monitored, so you take greater care in choosing your words. The newspapers you read are censored or banned. And after two months of serving this new regime, parliamentary democracy disappears.

If this were not enough, your position and purview are threatened by Party interlopers. Your authority is challenged as rival institutions are charged with handling aspects of foreign policy previously within your domain. And these ministries and their ministers are aggressively seeking control of the information they need to get ahead—and get you out.

And you face yet another dilemma. Your boss, the führer, holds his cards so close to his chest that you often don't know precisely what he wants. Wanting to serve your country and keep your job, you try to overcome this uncertainty by ascertaining the chancellor's will however you can, even circumventing standard operating procedures, withholding and manipulating information, and spying when you must.

In the back of your mind you worry that the Party might one day turn against you. Then, in the summer of 1934, after eighteen months of mounting tension, you witness the end of the rule of law. As thousands are arrested and an unknown number murdered, you soon learn that conservatives of your ilk are among the victims. Of the three most recent chancellors, you hear that one was shot to death in his home along with his wife. Another was placed under house arrest as his staff members were shot to death across their desks or sent to concentration camps. A third, you are told, fled into exile. And within your own ministry, colleagues are arrested and others are sent into hiding, fearing for their lives.

Then the situation worsens. Your government imposes racial purity laws, and some of your most trusted colleagues—the ones you counted on for information and support—are forced to resign, some left to flee the country, others doomed to concentration camps. Gestapo and SS intimidation intensify. By the end of 1938, an extraordinary outburst of violence sweeps across your country leaving thousands of German Jews dead, wounded, or arrested, synagogues and businesses burned to the ground— all under your government's watchful eye. And with each passing day, your country marches ever closer to the abyss of total war.

For much of the 1930s, Hitler enjoyed immense popularity. Torchlight parades, symbols of strength and unity, the restoration of German power and pride, all held tremendous appeal, not simply for the masses, but for the elites as well. Hitler's leading diplomats—the advisers he inherited from the Weimar regime and on whom he depended for continuity, intelligence, and knowledge of foreign capitals—shared many of the führer's broader political aims. They cheered the recapture of the Rhineland; they applauded the dismantling of the Versailles Treaty. They welcomed a return of Germany's rightful place as a great power and basked in Hitler's torchlit glory. This was one world in which the diplomats existed. It was the outer world, the one they could safely share with others. But below the surface of Germany's foreign policy successes lay a darker world, cast in the shadow of torchlight parades. And its climate was one of tension, uncertainty, and fear.

What Hitler Knew examines how governmental officials reached decisions on foreign policy under the stresses and strains of a violent dictatorship. It considers both the regime's domestic political environment and its control of information. Both are critical to understanding why Hitler made some of the key diplomatic and military decisions that have preoccupied historians for more than fifty years. Why did Stalin sign the Nazi-Soviet pact if he knew Hitler planned to invade? Why did Hitler risk a war with France in 1936 when Germany was almost certain to lose? Did British Prime Minister Neville Chamberlain actually seek a secret nonaggression pact with Hitler on the eve of war? As important as these questions are for an understanding of the period and the Cold War that followed, they are not the principal subjects of this book. Rather, they are the key moments through which decision making in Nazi Germany is examined.

What Hitler Knew asks upon what information Hitler's decisions were based. It attempts to determine what information his advisers brought him and what they manipulated or withheld altogether. Given that Hitler was not the sole decision maker in his regime, it also focuses on the diplomats who influenced Germany's foreign policy. How Foreign Ministry personnel, from Neurath to Ribbentrop, reached their own decisions is as much the subject of this study as is Hitler. Although at times it will be necessary to assess these men's own personal inclinations to determine how their respective ideologies and psychologies affected their behavior, the primary focus remains the manner in which they received, controlled, and forwarded information.

Information control exists in every regime, and in most bureaucracies information really does equal power. But in Hitler's Reich the near obsessive control of information held consequences for war and peace. Between 1933 and 1939, there was a gradual breakdown of traditional decision-making processes, yet this never reduced the advisers' influence. In fact, it increased it. Until the outbreak of war in 1939, with the signing of the Nazi-Soviet pact and the secret Anglo-German negotiations, Hitler's advisers manipulated policy by limiting what Hitler knew.

Ironically, Hitler's power to make informed decisions was limited by the very system he created. By rarely confiding in his advisers and by pitting each against the other, he produced a constant sense of uncertainty within the regime. Uncertainty grew to a climate of fear as state-sponsored violence and intimidation affected even the leading decision makers. Yet instead of making his advisers more cautious, the frenzied environment fostered greater risk. They tightened their grip on information and advocated more dangerous policies.

The reasons why Hitler's advisers exerted unusually strong control over the "information arsenal" (the cache of intelligence reports, sensitive diplomatic traffic, and other vital sources of information) are numerous. Sometimes they reacted to political rivalries, seeking to gain favor with the führer and outshine their colleagues. Sometimes they wanted to affect policy outcomes more in line with their individual worldviews. And sometimes they reacted out of fear. Whatever their motivations, they rose or fell in Hitler's Reich depending on how well they could wield the only weapon at their command—the knowledge they gathered from the documents that crossed their desks.

If the dictum "knowledge is power" contains any truth, then it must be equally true that lack of knowledge limits power. This is a book about power and its limitations. It is a study of how the control of knowledge—or information—affected decision making in Nazi Germany. And it is a portrait of how a dictator's seeming strength can actually be his weakest link.

The common perception of a dictator is of a man who rules with an iron fist. He decides independently what course he will take, he outlines policy, and his orders are obeyed. The actual power of a dictator, of course, is far more limited—limited in part by the information at his disposal. Once a leader ceases to make rational decisions, as was increasingly the case with Hitler during the war, the flow of information becomes far less relevant. So long as a leader operates with a semblance of rational thinking, as Hitler indeed did from 1933 to 1939, he remains constrained in part by what he knows. This is not to suggest that the more information an individual possesses, the better his decisions will necessarily be. However, the less he receives vital information, the more his options will be limited.

The book proceeds chronologically, exploring most of Hitler's major foreign policy decisions from the seizure of power to the outbreak of war. It investigates the background and motivations behind the alignment with Germany's sworn enemy Poland, the brazen and bloodless recapture of the Rhineland, the removal of Neurath and rise of Ribbentrop, the secret Anglo-German nonaggression pact talks, and the internal intrigues behind the Nazi-Soviet pact. Each case study highlights the role of information flow and the domestic political environment for their impact on each decision's outcome. The book draws on a range of sources from several countries and languages, including newly available KGB archives and records from the former East Germany.

One of the challenges for any study of Nazi Germany is to explain why, given the Third Reich's brutal nature, the non-Nazi diplomats continued to serve. It is impossible to reconstitute all the influences that affected decision makers. How can the historian know of the important telephone call about which Neurath made no record but which shaped his position on a particular issue, or of the hushed conversation made in ministry corridors that no one chose to record, or of the incriminating document that someone deliberately destroyed? Undoubtedly, some continued to serve because they agreed with Hitler's general aims: revision of Versailles, reduction of Poland, and the restoration of German power. But even given their general agreement, their continued support seems odd in light of state-sponsored terror, and especially after the murder and arrest of many of their own colleagues during the "Night of the Long Knives" in 1934. Some surely believed that they could act as breaks on the regime's excesses or could steer it in the proper direction. This they could only do from within the government, since opposition from without appeared futile. Some must have felt beholden to principles of duty and service to the Fatherland and believed that resignation would be a betrayal of this sacred oath. Or is that how they rationalized their inability to resign in protest? Still others came gradually, and far more gradually than one might expect, to sabotage the regime, and some of these men paid with their lives.

But what of the others, those who neither condoned Nazi brutality nor tried to sabotage it? What kept them on? The first chapter asks how Germany came to form an agreement with its hated rival, Poland, and why the men in the Foreign Ministry supported it. As events with Poland and Soviet Russia unfolded, Hitler's advisers were acting under an expanding cloud of violence, intimidation, and fear. To understand why they acted as they did, you must now place yourself within Hitler's darker world.

Hitler's Opening Gambit
Intelligence, Fear, and the German-Polish Agreement

1

Why did Germany align with Poland, its detested neighbor? In the eyes of many Germans, including the diplomats, Poland was a hated reminder of their loss in World War I, created by the Allies out of German territory, and the notion of an alliance with the Poles was repugnant to them. Yet when Hitler in his first year as chancellor turned Germany's eastern alliances on their head, dropping the Soviet ally, the Weimar era diplomats fell into line. Why did Foreign Ministry officials seem to change their views so dramatically on this cornerstone of German foreign policy?

Within one month of coming to power, Hitler initiated mass arrests of Communists and Socialists, in a "mini-wave of terror" — "mini" insofar as it was a small sample of the terror to come.[1] The burning of the Reichstag building on the night of February 27 released the floodgates of terror. Standing outside the burning building, and accusing the Communists of starting the blaze, Hitler shrieked uncontrollably:

> There will be no mercy now. Anyone who stands in our way will be cut down. The German people will not tolerate leniency. Every Communist official will be shot where he is found. The Communist deputies must be hanged this very night. Everybody in league with

the Communists must be arrested. There will no longer be any le-
niency for the Social Democrats either.[2]

Within the next two years some 60,000 Germans would be arrested and
nearly 2,000 killed.[3]

One month later, Hitler gained near dictatorial powers through the
Enabling Act, having co-opted the Catholic Center Party with promises to
protect their religious freedom. Only the Social Democrats (SPD) voted
against it. On March 24, 1933, Germany's experiment with democracy col-
lapsed, and with it ended the freedoms that the German people — and the
conservative diplomats — had experienced for the previous fourteen years.

The diary of Viktor Klemperer, a Jewish professor in Dresden, helps
to convey the nation's darkening mood.

> March 22, 1933: Fraülein Wiechmann visited us. She tells how in her
> school in Meissen all are bowing down to the swastika, are trembling
> for their jobs, watching and distrusting one another. A young man
> with a swastika comes into the school on some official errand or
> other. A class of fourteen-year-olds immediately begins singing the
> Horst Wessel Song. Singing in the corridor is not allowed. Fraülein
> Wiechmann is on duty. "You must forbid this bawling," urge her col-
> leagues. — "You do it then. If I forbid *this* bawling, it will be said
> that I have taken action against the national song, and I will be out
> on my ear." The girls go on bawling. — In a pharmacy, toothpaste
> with the swastika. — A mood of fear such as must have existed in
> France under the Jacobins. No one fears for their lives yet, but for
> bread and freedom.[4]

> May 15, 1933: Everywhere complete helplessness, cowardice, and
> fear. . . . The garden of a Communist in Heidenau is dug up. There
> is supposed to be a machine-gun in it. Nothing is found. To squeeze
> a confession out of him he is beaten to death. The corpse brought to
> the hospital. Boot marks on the stomach. Fist-sized holes in the
> back. . . . Post-mortem results: cause of death dysentery.[5]

A climate of distrust among neighbors, colleagues, friends, and even
within families emerged from fear of being denounced. And not only enemies of the state were at risk. The physician son of one of Klemperer's
friends was imprisoned because letters of his had been found in the home

of a Communist. Imagine the maddening uncertainty that ordinary Germans must have experienced as they wondered what evidence might be found that could place them or their families in jeopardy.

The diplomats were no more immune to the climate of fear than any other Germans. In fact, many had greater cause for concern as most of the upper-level officials were not Nazi Party members. Rather, the Weimar-era diplomats were drawn from an elite social class and had trained in a ministry with a rich and rigid tradition. As Peter Krüger has observed in his thorough study of the ministry's social composition, "even after 1918/1919 and the constitutional changes, and after the abolishing of a privileged nobility as a state, the model of aristocratic duty to the state and monarchy remained alive."[6] Ministry officials were among the most educated and privileged men in society, and they viewed service to the state as a responsibility of their rank. Even among the other government ministries, the Foreign Ministry held a position of prominence and prestige.[7]

The ministry's organization followed rigid lines of hierarchical command, whereby a rational bureaucratic structure divided labor into political, commercial, and legal affairs, with the political division being the most prestigious. In 1920, Edmund Schüler, a member of the ministry's personnel department, spearheaded a series of reforms to modernize the ministry and alter its organization to allow for greater influence of new élites. As a result, an expanding middle class of entrepreneurs and professionals was brought in to handle the pressing reparations and disarmament issues after World War I. Despite these reforms, the aristocratic nobility still held a dominant position over political decision making.

While a hierarchical structure existed under the Weimar-era ministry, high-level officials could disagree and not suffer extreme consequences. For example, Foreign Minister Gustav Stresemann's policy of "fulfillment" emphasized cooperation with the Allies, whereas Ambassador Constantin Freiherr von Neurath held more nationalistic views and often found himself in opposition to the foreign minister's policies.[8] While Neurath expressed his differences with his chief, he never had reason to fear a violent reprisal from the state for espousing his views.

After Stresemann's death in 1929, there was a noticeable shift to the right in the ministry's personnel, giving the Wilhelmstraße a more nationalistic character. Under Heinrich Brüning's chancellorship, the ministry's long-time state secretary, Carl von Schubert, was demoted to ambassador and sent to Rome. Bernhard Wilhelm von Bülow, nephew of the former chancellor, was appointed in his place. And with Neurath's ascension to the foreign minister's post, the ministry's face changed substantially.

Following the Machtergreifung, the aristocratic diplomats found the social composition of the Wilhelmstraße once more under siege. Just as the Schüler reforms had resulted in the diffusion of some power to new élites, the conservatives now had to defend their position against Nazi Party intruders, who typically represented less educated, less worldly men from lower economic and social strata. But these challenges to their social composition from within the ministry were intensified by the system of overlapping institutions Hitler created, each of which laid claim to part of the diplomats' domain.

The traditional instrument for determining Germany's foreign policy had been the Foreign Ministry (in German the Auswärtiges Amt, abbreviated AA, located in the Wilhelmstraße 74-76, and thus often referred to simply as the Wilhelmstraße). After Hitler seized power, Alfred Rosenberg seemed poised to replace the aristocratic Neurath as foreign minister. Rosenberg had served the Nazi Party as its chief authority on foreign affairs, having published a book in 1927 on Germany's new course in the international arena. But President von Hindenburg insisted on preserving Neurath in his post. When Hitler spoke of making Rosenberg the ministry's state secretary, the foreign minister objected and the idea was dropped. Hitler did not possess the power in 1933 to override both the president's and the foreign minister's wishes on personnel matters. On April 1, 1933, Hitler created the Außenpolitisches Amt (APA), to serve as the party's foreign policy wing, placing Rosenberg at its head.[9] But the APA failed to affect German foreign policy directly and Rosenberg never achieved a position of influence commensurate with his ambitions.

Several other governmental organizations quickly arose, seeking to imprint Nazism on Germany's foreign policy. On May 8, 1933, Ernst Bohle was named head of the Auslandsorganisation (AO), responsible for Germans living outside the Reich. In addition to the AO, the Volksdeutsche Rat (VR), established on October 27, 1933, was responsible for Germans living abroad who did not possess German citizenship, but who, because of their ancestry and language, belonged culturally to the German Reich. Finally, the Büro Ribbentrop, created on April 24, 1934, which became the Dienststelle Ribbentrop on June 1, 1935, served as Joachim von Ribbentrop's personal office, assisting him in executing the special missions the führer assigned him. Each of the four new institutions, led by ambitious men, struggled to gain access to the information essential to conducting policy.

Whereas Rosenberg sought direct control over foreign affairs, Hermann Göring followed a more subtle yet insidious path to power. In June 1933, Göring attempted to create a German central intelligence agency that would intercept all police, military, and diplomatic telegrams, giving him full and unrestricted access to vital information. Neurath understandably rejected this proposal and succeeded in thwarting its implementation.

Although he failed in this initial effort, Göring did manage to create a wire-tapping bureau (Forschungsamt), which often intercepted the cables and telephone conversations of foreign and German officials. Established to discover Nazi enemies, the intrusive instrument produced caution and fear among many, but it did not halt all risky communication. In May 1934, just prior to the Röhm purge, Joachim von Ribbentrop held numerous lengthy and secret conversations with foreign representatives in Geneva. But those calls did not remain secret for very long. Erich Kordt, the ministry official assigned to "assist" Ribbentrop, reported that "a few hours after one such telephone conversation, a verbatim text appeared on my desk from Göring's wire-tapping service." Although in this instance the information aided the Foreign Ministry, Kordt soberly noted that Göring's surveillance system "brought many who had conducted an ill-thought-out telephone conversation to their doom."[10]

Göring's Gestapo and Forschungsamt tactics threatened the free flow of information, as diplomats and Nazi leaders had to become more cautious in their conduct of daily business, but his forays into foreign affairs had little direct impact on actual policy in the early years.[11]

Dr. Joseph Goebbels also made an early bid for information control. His original intent was to seize control of the Foreign Ministry's Press Division, but Neurath fended off this attempt. Goebbels did manage to intervene in foreign affairs during the initial stages of the Nazi regime, but he quickly receded into domestic affairs as his Ministry for Public Enlightenment and Propaganda consumed his activities.

A more problematic challenge arose from the AO's Ernst Bohle. In 1934, Alfred Rosenberg attempted to absorb the AO into his own Party office, but Bohle parried Rosenberg's attack by placing the AO under the control of Rudolf Hess, the chancellor's deputy, and thereby retained some autonomy.

The AO initially proved troublesome to Neurath, who received complaints from diplomats in foreign countries being harassed by AO officials seeking to exert Nazi Party authority over them. In February 1936, following the murder of Wilhelm Gustloff, the AO chief in Switzerland, Hitler considered closing the organization. On February 27, in an aggressive attempt to preserve his influence and curtail Neurath's, Bohle proposed that the führer elevate his rank to state secretary for the AO and permit him to operate his organization from within the Foreign Ministry. Despite obtaining Hess's approval, Bohle failed to gain Hitler's consent and, although it did become absorbed into the Foreign Ministry in January 1937, the AO never again seriously threatened Neurath or his conduct of foreign policy.[12]

While these many alternative institutions never directly influenced the issues of greatest importance, they did have an *indirect* effect on policy because they compelled Foreign Ministry officials to protect and defend their influence. Because their power stemmed overwhelmingly from the information they controlled, and because their rivals constantly sought to wrest that information from them, the diplomats developed a near obsessive need to control the information flow. Germany's tense relations with Poland in 1933 reveal how information — and in particular secret intelligence — had assumed an even more vital role.

Although Hitler did not possess detailed blueprints for conducting Germany's foreign policy, he did hold consistently to certain ideological beliefs. As far as Ostpolitik was concerned, Hitler's general intentions are clear: the destruction of Versailles' territorial arrangements; an expansion of the Reich eastward to obtain Lebensraum; and the subjugation of the Slav race, the Untermenschen he so despised.

Hitler wrote remarkably little about a specific Polish policy in *Mein Kampf*. But in his secret second book, the one he never intended for publication, he referred more frequently to the Poles, yet still did not directly mention forming a pact with them. In one chapter, however, Hitler did spell out eight principles for Germany's foreign policy. After noting that Germany could not hope to change her situation through the League of Nations because the victor states were committed to keeping Germany weak, Hitler asserted that Germany must regain military strength, must not come into conflict with the French alliance system surrounding Germany, and could not form an alliance system with states whose ultimate foreign policy aims were in contradiction to Germany's. Given these principles, it is possible that Hitler had Poland already in mind as a would-be ally. His fifth principle, however, which concerned potential partners, foreshadowed the later accord.

> Germany cannot hope that these states can be found outside the League of Nations. On the contrary her only hope must consist in her eventual success in extricating individual states from the coalition of victor states and building a new group of interested parties with new aims which cannot be realized through the League of Nations because of its whole nature.[13]

Hitler's racist views toward the Poles naturally colored his view of any potential agreement with them:

> The folkish state, conversely, must under no conditions annex Poles with the intention of wanting to make Germans out of them. On the contrary it must muster the determination either to seal off these alien racial elements, so that the blood of its own people will not be corrupted again, or it must without further ado remove them and hand over the vacated territory to its own national comrades.[14]

Many Germans feared a Polish attack in the east, especially because Germany's military forces were restricted by the terms of Versailles. Rumors and angst over such an attack surfaced from time to time in the 1920s, as did occasional border clashes.[15] Growing Polish nationalism gave many Germans reason to be anxious about their eastern neighbor. Nationalistic tendencies may have been particularly strong in part because ethnic Poles comprised only 68.9 percent of the population. In many areas of Poland, minority ethnic groups constituted a majority.[16] Poland's invasion of the Ukraine in 1920–21, coupled with the aggressiveness of Poland's strong-handed leader, Marshal Jósef Pilsudski, who assumed power in 1926 by means of a coup d'état, did little to alleviate German concerns.

The fear of being attacked, combined with resentment over Versailles' restrictions and racist anti-Polish sentiments, led German statesmen— Stresemann primary among them[17]—to strive for clandestine rearmament throughout the 1920s. The Rapallo agreement, concluded in secret during the Genoa conference in 1922, satisfied this ambition. Rapallo provided for mutual assistance between the two "pariah" states, Germany and Soviet Russia, whereby each agreed to cancel the other's debts, to return to normal diplomatic relations, and to increase trade.[18] More important, the agreement enabled German troops to train secretly on Russian terrain and permitted German industries such as Krupp Steel and Junker aircraft manufacturers to produce war materiel under the opaque Soviet cloak. Its wider impact, however, was to wreck the Genoa conference and then to strain Germany's relations with the other European states.[19]

Whatever damage Rapallo might have caused to Germany's relations with the West, the agreement with Russia also satisfied anti-Polish sentiments, especially within the army. General Hans von Seeckt, head of the Reichswehr, had been working for military cooperation with Soviet Russia as early as 1920−21. Without informing the Foreign Ministry, Seeckt sent his personal representative, Colonel Walther Nicolai, who had served as head of the German secret service during World War I, to Moscow. His mission was to lay the groundwork for military discussions about which even the civilian heads of state in Germany were to be kept ignorant.[20] After Rapallo was concluded, Seeckt articulated his anti-Polish views in a memorandum on September 11, 1922.

> Poland's existence is intolerable, incompatible with the survival of Germany. It must disappear, and it will disappear through its internal weakness and through Russia—with our assistance. . . . With Poland falls one of the strongest pillars of the Treaty of Versailles, the preponderance of France. . . . Poland can never offer any advantage to Germany, either economically, because it is incapable of any development, or politically, because it is France's vassal. The reestablishment of the broad common frontier between Russia and Germany is the precondition for the regaining of strength of both countries.[21]

Most diplomats in the German Foreign Ministry shared Seeckt's and Hitler's animosity toward the Poles, though they may not have agreed with Hitler's racial fanaticism. The diplomats, especially those who had fought in World War I, resented the loss of former German territory to the Poles and hoped for a revision of boundaries. Many viewed Poland's treatment

of its German minority as oppressive. By 1933, the fear of a Polish attack
had risen substantially, and the diplomats were forced to react.

As early as January 19, 1933 Bülow recorded a war scare in the air. The
German ambassador to France, Count Johannes von Welczeck, informed
Bülow of steady rumors in Paris about the inevitability of a German-
Polish conflict and information he received that Poland would attack Germany and Danzig in the near future.[22] On February 8, a German official,
Theodore von Bibenstein, telegraphed State Secretary Otto Meissner to
report on Polish plans to exploit Germany's present weakness. According
to Bibenstein's sources, the Polish government intended to instigate an uprising of the Polish minority living in Germany's eastern provinces under
the pretext that they could no longer live under the German yoke.[23]
Whether Meissner took seriously Bibenstein's information and whether it
had a direct impact on foreign policy is not important; its significance lies
in the fact that it represents part of a mounting anxiety over Polish aggression. It is this fear that would lead to a decisive change in policy.

German perceptions of Poland's military build-up were further fueled
by the Westerplatte incident in early March. In an attempted demonstration of strength, Pilsudski sent a transport to the Danzig harbor, reinforcing the guards at munitions stores by 125 men. This was a clear violation of
an agreement from 1925, and it only served to intensify anti-Polish sentiment within Germany and the international community. It probably also
strengthened the hand of the Danzig Nazis. In mid-March, Hitler informed the cabinet that he had instructed the Danzig Nazis to halt their demands for new elections,[24] but for reasons that are unclear, by April 3, the
führer appears to have changed his mind. Neurath told Ernst Ziehm, head
of the Nationalist Danzig Senate, to dissolve the Volkstag and call for new
elections. This resulted in a dramatic victory for the Nazis, who won 50.3
percent of the popular vote and secured an absolute majority of seats.[25]

With relations worsening, Neurath unequivocally rejected any alignment with Poland. On April 7, he told the cabinet:

> An understanding with Poland is neither possible nor desirable. We
> must maintain a certain amount of German-Polish tension in order to
> interest the rest of the world in our revisionist demands and in order
> to keep Poland economically and politically weak. The situation is in

no way without danger, since the present Polish government is apparently playing with the idea of a preventive war, in the knowledge that the progressive strengthening of Germany will only impair her prospects and reduce France's allegiance to the alliance.[26]

Intelligence continued to reach the German Foreign Ministry regarding Polish military preparations. On April 12, Georg Martius, special adviser to the Foreign Ministry, telegraphed the foreign minister, the state secretary, and the heads of all the ministry's departments to pass on secret military reports from Warsaw of an alleged meeting between the Soviet ambassador and Pilsudski.[27] This hinted at Polish-Soviet cooperation, precisely the scenario that the German Foreign Ministry came increasingly to suspect and fear.

Another report noted that Polish war preparations were evident from trends in industrial activity. A one hundred percent increase in war industry production was under way: airplane motors, munitions, field cookers, gas protection devices, grain stocks, magazines, as well as increased dealings with France for artillery contracts.[28]

An even more disturbing cable soon arrived from Gottfried Aschmann, the Foreign Ministry's Press Division chief. Although reports from the Press Division did not take precedence over those from ambassadors or envoys, Aschmann's contacts were considerable and his information reliable. On April 20, Aschmann sent a top secret report labeled "Poland's Plan for Occupation of Danzig," which gave detailed intelligence:

> In the event of expected Nazi actions relating to elections in Senate, Polish General Staff expects to use three infantry divisions, two cavalry brigades, who will be strengthened by the requisite technical and artillery troops made doubly large. The air force will not be necessary until the moment when a full conflict erupts between Germany and Poland. The whole operation should take on the appearance of a police action for restoration of order and re-control of ports. No mobilization is planned unless conflict with German troops occurs. In contrast to Polish Foreign Ministry opinion the Polish General Staff is "fully convinced" that Germany will take no steps which could lead to war with Poland and will seek to resolve the conflict through diplomatic measures. As far as the General Staff understands the French position and view of the French public, it [the general staff]

takes the position that "Poland may in no case be the aggressor," and therefore it is wished to avoid an expansion of the planned action. The solution to the Upper Silesian problem should be postponed to a more appropriate time, which they believe will soon come in Germany.[29]

Even if Aschmann's information had been planted by the Poles as a counter to aggressive Nazi activities in Danzig, the impact upon the Foreign Ministry was real. Similar reports continued to stream in from a variety of sources. On April 22, the German ambassador in Rome, Ulrich von Hassell, wired the Foreign Ministry that former Reich chancellor Joseph Wirth had learned from sources close to the Czechoslovak government of aggressive Polish intentions on Germany's eastern front supported by Prague.[30] After receiving Hassell's intelligence, State Secretary von Bülow cabled the war minister, von Blomberg, requesting additional military intelligence.[31] The Foreign Ministry's unease waxed when on April 25, the German ambassador in Warsaw, Helmuth von Moltke, cabled Berlin that war appeared likely.[32] That same day Berlin received similar warnings from another ministry official.[33] The following day the Foreign Ministry issued an alert to its embassies in Warsaw, Moscow, Geneva, Rome, and London, warning that a Polish preemptive strike appeared imminent.[34]

Concomitant with reports over Polish war preparations came increasing intelligence on covert Polish-Soviet negotiations. On April 29, von Moltke wired Berlin on signs of an improvement in Polish-Russian relations. Moltke noted that the publisher of the *Gazetta Polska*, a parliamentarian of the government's party, Mr. Miedzynski, was traveling to Moscow, apparently as a response to the previous year's visit of the foreign policy editor of *Izvestiya*, Mr. Rayevsky. Moltke wrote, "It is safe to assume that Miedzynski has gone to Moscow for the purpose of forming a Polish-Russian understanding. The development of Polish-Russian relations proceeds at an ever increasing tempo whereby the Polish government is the driving force while the Soviet regime is more reserved and reluctant."[35]

Hitler received the Polish ambassador on May 2 and told him that Germany could never accept the present arrangement over Danzig. The Polish representative responded that since Hitler assumed power, Polish-German relations had deteriorated markedly. Poland needed Danzig for access to the sea. Hitler insisted he could never grant this special right to

Poland. Versailles, he continued, had been constructed by shortsighted politicians, and as long as the current borders existed, tension with Poland would continue.[36] Ten days later, Bibenstein sent word to Berlin that two-thirds of Polish forces now stood along a well-fortified western frontier and were not being recalled.[37]

As tensions heightened over a possible Polish preventive war, the Foreign Ministry became aware of a new development that threatened to isolate Germany still further and leave her highly vulnerable. The Wilhelmstraße's officials had learned of secret negotiations between the Poles, Soviets, and Romanians. If such a constellation were to form, Germany would find herself at best severely isolated, at worst open to attack.

The official charged with investigating the possible alliance was the German ambassador in Moscow, Herbert von Dirksen. Ambassador Dirksen was one of the ministry's most able men. He had previously served as the consul general in Warsaw, was highly educated, possessing a doctoral degree in law, spoke several languages fluently, and enjoyed the respect and friendship of most of his colleagues. Richard Meyer, the chief of the Foreign Ministry's Political Division, informed Dirksen that the Polish government intended to send its second special mission to Moscow in the near future and the selection of delegates indicated the mission's serious nature. Meyer added, "We have reason to believe that the Soviet Union is seeking some sort of agreement with the Polish government."[38]

Dirksen encountered only evasiveness from Soviet officials. Boris Stomonyakov, Dirksen's Soviet interlocutor, denied any knowledge of the talks being reported in the Polish press. He dismissed speculations that Mr. Miedzynski had visited the Moscow Foreign Ministry and claimed that the sole Polish politician to have visited Moscow was Oberst Schaetzel, chief of the Eastern Division in the Polish Foreign Office. When Dirksen probed deeper, asking whether any discussions were currently taking place, Stomonyakov replied that only a technical agreement was being discussed involving the transportation of timber through riverways. In contrast to official Soviet stonewalling, Dirksen said he had learned from a highly reliable source that the negotiations had indeed taken place. They had broken off when Poland made its agreement to Soviet proposals contingent on obtaining a similar agreement with Romania.

Given the matter's gravity, not only were the foreign minister and state secretary sent copies of Dirksen's report, but the chiefs of all ministry de-

partments received this information as well.[39] Back in Berlin, Bülow awaited
verification of the clandestine negotiations. When Dirksen's cable arrived
on May 15, he immediately sent copies to the German ambassadors in
Paris and Bucharest in hope of obtaining further information about the
French and Romanian governments' activities.[40]

It is impossible to establish precisely when Hitler decided to pursue a
Polish agreement. In his postwar memoirs, Ambassador von Dirksen recalled a meeting in early May 1933 with the führer in which Hitler told him
that he wanted friendly relations with Russia. As Dirksen wrote: "But
then something happened which I will never forget. He [Hitler] raised himself, went to the window, and said dreamily, 'If only we could have good relations with Poland, but Pilsudski is the only person who can do that.'"
Hitler said no more to Dirksen about it.[41] This exchange suggests that
Hitler did have the changing of Germany's eastern policy in mind early on
in 1933. However, at that time, Hitler was primarily concerned with con-
solidating his power. He was not yet head of state, nor had he fully established a dictatorship. He was preoccupied with domestic concerns, imple-
menting anti-Socialist and anti-Communist policies, such as outlawing the
Communist party, arresting its leader, Ernst Thalmann, and closing socialist presses. In the process of creating a one-party state, he also had to
determine how to deal with Ernst Röhm and the Sturmabteilung (SA).
Since Hitler did not command unquestioning loyalty or admiration from
his non-Nazi Foreign Ministry, why did Foreign Ministry officials support
such a radical shift so early on in the Nazi regime?

In State Secretary Bülow's conception of Germany's eastern policy,
Germany's prime security concerns revolved around France and Poland.
He saw Germany's security from French aggression as guaranteed by Locarno, but protection from a Polish attack came through the Russian cover
in the rear. Good relations with the Soviet Union were therefore essential.
As he phrased it, Germany was secure so long as the Soviets could march
on Poland's eastern border. For this reason it was not necessary to align
with Poland in order to separate her from France.

But Bülow feared Germany's encirclement. Such a possibility was to
be avoided at all cost until Germany had rearmed, and he estimated that
the country required roughly five years to return to a position of strength
with respect to her neighbors. Above all, Germany required peace in order
to rearm. But Bülow recognized that Poland was contemplating a preven-

tive war.[42] Without a period of peace, Germany could neither rearm nor pursue her revisionist aims. The maintenance of good relations with the Soviets was also vital, but this depended on a reciprocal Soviet desire. Once Bülow learned of the clandestine Soviet attempts at alliance with Poland, his carefully planned policies had to be revised. In the absence of a Soviet cover in the east, German security required reinforcement. An alternative alignment needed to be made and the options were few. Unfortunately, his calculations had to be made under increasing pressure from within the regime.

While straining to defuse highly combustible Polish-German relations in early 1933, Bülow and his Foreign Ministry colleagues suddenly found themselves the focus of state police scrutiny. On March 10, Richard Meyer of the Political Division received a confidential report over a recent police action. In the preceding weeks, secret police had arrested some twenty individuals on charges of spying and high treason. These people were allegedly involved in a Polish spy ring engaged in industrial espionage for the Polish Air Force. Those arrested included high-profile members of Germany's élite, such as the son of the famed World War I hero General Erich von Falkenhayn, and prominent industrialists, such as Joseph von Berg, director of Siemens' Air Armaments Division.[43]

This episode further strained already tense German-Polish relations. And because one of those arrested was a Foreign Ministry official, Bülow and his associates fell under increased police scrutiny. Making matters worse, the police failed to consult with any Foreign Ministry officials prior to making the arrests, despite the issue's significance for German-Polish relations. Recognizing that widespread knowledge of the spy ring could prove detrimental, Goebbels' Propaganda Ministry forbade any mention of the affair in the media, and thus few knew of its occurrence or import, but the matter did not disappear.

Germany's evolving Polish policy developed an increasingly complex nature. On the one hand, Hitler and Foreign Ministry officials seemed to agree that a strong line on Danzig was necessary. Yet the matter could not be pushed too far lest Germany provoke a Polish assault for which the Reich was wholly unprepared. Fears of isolation and encirclement demanded that some measures be undertaken to prevent a hostile coalition from forming on Germany's eastern flank. National Socialist rhetoric and German national pride, however, required a firm stand on Danzig.

Frustrated over the difficulties in pursuing a coherent German foreign policy while Nazi domestic policies worked against his efforts, the state secretary contemplated relinquishing his post. In a draft of a resignation letter from May or early June, Bülow wrote: "Our behavior towards Poland, especially that of the National Socialists in Danzig, has raised the danger of a war with our unsettled Polish neighbor, a conflict for which we are neither militarily nor in other respects sufficiently strong." He continued that only a harmonizing of domestic with foreign policy could enable Germany to parry the dangers posed to its security. "If such a harmonizing does not occur," Bülow asserted, "I can no longer maintain my post." At first Bülow included the names of Germany's ambassadors in London, Paris, and Moscow (his close friends Leopold von Hoesch, Roland Köster, and Dirksen), claiming to be writing on their behalf as well. He then scratched out the sentence, perhaps deciding that he needed to perform this act alone.[44]

Bülow never submitted that resignation letter. Instead, he continued to serve as state secretary until his death in 1936. Beyond the inner turmoil that this draft letter reveals, it also demonstrates that he considered peace with Poland essential. The ongoing conflicts, war scares, and deteriorating relations with Soviet Russia necessitated a shift in relations in order to preserve the peace and allow rearmament to continue.

Throughout 1933, the Soviets became increasingly disenchanted with their erstwhile German partner. One factor that heightened Soviet mistrust and desire for revision of its security agreements was the infamous Hugenberg Memorandum. At the world economic conference held in London in the summer of 1933, Cabinet Minister Alfred Hugenberg, acting independently, called for a division of Russia and the Ukraine. Although this debacle led to Hugenberg's dismissal, the Soviets drew nearer to concluding that Hitler's anti-Bolshevik, anti-Slavic rhetoric represented a serious German policy. Hitler's termination of military cooperation with the Soviet Red Army further bolstered their suspicions.[45]

Although the Polish war scare subsided in May, there would be little peace for the Foreign Ministry. While an immediate Polish attack had been avoided, relations remained tense. On July 13, Hitler again received the Polish ambassador and reaffirmed his aversion to war and support of Poland's right to exist.[46] Such diplomatic platitudes did not yet draw Pilsudski into negotiations with Germany. For the German Foreign Ministry, the danger of a Polish-Soviet alliance still loomed ominously.

The most troubling information of that summer came from the German military attaché in Warsaw. Herr Schindler reported on July 19 that Poland had been delivering war planes to Romania.[47] That same day Schindler cabled Berlin of rumors that the heads of the Polish, Romanian, and French air forces were meeting to discuss the coordination of joint operations.[48] The military attaché confidently asserted that such rumors should not be taken seriously. But soon thereafter he was impelled to change his mind. On August 3, Schindler sent a detailed report to both the Foreign Ministry and the Reichswehr Ministry entitled "Changes in Poland's Political-Military Situation," in which he assessed Poland's closening ties with Soviet Russia and her increasingly anti-German position.

Schindler noted that Karl Radek and two prominent Soviet fighter pilots had recently visited Poland, and he interpreted this as a clear sign of growing closeness. Schindler insisted that because Poland's relations with Soviet Russia and her other potential opponents had improved, the pressure on her eastern flank had been freed. In response, Schindler believed, Poland was certain to turn her military toward Germany.

> It will be unavoidable that in the next few years the Polish army will see Germany as its sole adversary and will adjust its preparations accordingly. . . . The great relaxation in the east, the improvement in military organization and training, the increasingly anti-German stance, the friendship with France, the good relations with Czechoslovakia, will create, not only for the military leaders but also for the leader of the state, a great temptation to use these advantageous circumstances for a military success and an expansion of Polish power. It is known that Pilsudski himself is not anti-German and that he does not aim at a war with Germany. But neither as a soldier nor as a statesman could he afford to miss an opportunity for a success for his country.[49]

With such disturbing information from their military attaché, the diplomats had to be concerned. If Schindler's analysis proved correct, Germany would find herself facing an aggressive threat to the east without the essential Soviet cover.

In September, the threat of a Polish-Soviet alliance reached its zenith. On September 5 the Foreign Ministry cabled its embassies in Moscow and Warsaw that Pilsudski had allegedly received an invitation to visit the Soviet government. The newspaper *Deutsche Rundschau* in Poland published a story asserting that it was highly possible that the marshal would go to Moscow to discuss Eastern Europe, citing as its source the American publisher Tomaacz Siomiradzki, known to be close to Pilsudski.[50]

Alerted to the dangers of a Polish-Soviet alliance, a ministry official in Washington, DC, Leitner, drew the Foreign Ministry's attention to an article in the *New York Times*, also reprinted in Britain's *Daily Herald* and Poland's Socialist *Robotnik*. The *Times* reported on secret negotiations currently taking place in Zaleszczyki between high-ranking officials of the Polish, Soviet, and Romanian governments. Pilsudski was allegedly already in attendance and was soon to be joined by Foreign Minister Józef Beck, as well as several officials from the Polish Foreign Ministry. Marshal K. E. Voroshilov, the Soviet war minister, was also expected. Together with the Romanian premier, these governments intended to form an anti-German eastern front.[51]

How seriously did the Wilhelmstraße take these rumors circulating in the foreign presses? One indication is that the foreign minister, state secretary, and all department heads received copies of Leitner's report. In an effort to stem domestic concerns and a further deterioration in Polish relations, Goebbels' Propaganda Ministry forbade any comment on the matter in the German press, insisting that the reports of secret talks were untrue.[52] Yet despite the official assurances, Germany began serious efforts to improve relations rapidly throughout the ensuing weeks.

Even if the suspected talks were only rumors, they reflected a deeply disturbing situation. The threat of a Polish-Soviet-Romanian coalition, coupled with uncertain relations with the Western Powers, brought home to the Foreign Ministry the danger of Germany's position. The estrangement of Soviet Russia had fueled speculation over German encirclement and isolation, and such a scenario had to be avoided.

Unfortunately for the Foreign Ministry, the reports of covert talks in the east coincided with growing internal pressure on ministry officials. On September 11, the ministry's Political Division chief received renewed demands from both the secret police and Abwehr for the release and publication of details surrounding the Polish spy ring. With the forthcoming disarmament conference on the horizon, the police and army sought to gain political capital and a relaxation in arms limitations by exposing Polish machinations to the world. The Foreign Ministry again resisted this pressure, knowing that publication of facts about the spy ring would only exacerbate the delicate situation.

The following day, as Bülow obtained Meyer's report on the matter, the Reichswehr repeated its demand for immediate publication. In order to underscore the matter's importance, a police representative visited the Wilhelmstraße to pressure the Foreign Ministry still further. Fearing that Poland might be on the verge of an anti-German alliance with the Soviets and Romanians, the Foreign Ministry had no option other than to reject these attempts to manipulate foreign policy, especially at such a critical moment. Goebbels' suppression of any reporting on the spy ring helped check the police's and military's intrusions,[53] but even Goebbels' press censorship could not prevent rumors from circulating at such a tense time in German-Polish relations.

Back in Warsaw, Schindler had to learn of the espionage affair from a Polish army officer. He heard that the Polish military attaché in Berlin had been accused of involvement in a spy ring, but the details of the entire episode had been shrouded in confusion and hearsay. Embarrassed that he had to learn of events from the Poles, Schindler wired Berlin on September 20 requesting that he be immediately informed.[54]

Just two weeks after Leitner's report, Polish Foreign Minister Beck came to Berlin for meetings with Neurath and Goebbels. On September 26, the three men discussed ways of relaxing tensions between their two nations and proposed the standard precursors to political agreement: a cessation of mutual press attacks and an improvement in economic ties. Negotiations were to commence in Berlin on October 3.[55] The Foreign Ministry was now committed to the new course.

As often occurred in Nazi Germany during times of transition and uncertainty in foreign affairs, amateurs emerged to play a part in negotiations. On October 5, one unlikely interloper, a corporate leader named Hahn,[56] met with Foreign Minister Beck for three hours in a Geneva hotel room to discuss German-Polish relations in detail. Speaking in French without interpreters present, Beck and Hahn outlined the principal sticking points requiring resolution. Beck repeatedly stressed his disappointment with the League of Nations in settling conflicts and insisted that any understanding between their countries would have to be bilateral. No intervention by a third party was acceptable to him. The main point, Hahn related in his lengthy report to Neurath, was Beck's desire for a genuine improvement in relations. Hahn's memorandum was sent again to the state secretary and all department heads.[57]

During the next few days, attempts at closer economic relations ran into some difficulty over coal exports from Upper Silesia, and Neurath feared the talks would fail. Hitler, however, urged making concessions to Poland in order to bring the new relationship with Poland to fruition.[58]

On October 14, Hitler executed his first "Saturday Surprise" by withdrawing Germany from the League of Nations and the Disarmament Conference. In an almost ritual practice, the chancellor followed his announcement with a public overture for peace, in this instance calling for Franco-German friendship and direct negotiations. Hitler instructed General Werner von Blomberg to prepare for military sanctions, yet none was forthcoming. President Franklin Roosevelt openly opposed American sanctions on Germany and the other Western Powers proved divided.[59] Hitler's disruption of the League would proceed by drawing Poland into direct alignment.

On October 17, the Danzig Nazi leader, Hermann Rauschning, received the führer's instruction for the Danzig senate to reach accord with Poland in all areas, "insofar as this could possibly be done without imperiling the German character of Danzig and German interests."[60] The following day, Poland's new ambassador to Berlin, Jozef Lipski, who was widely seen as a rising star in the Polish diplomatic corps, presented his credentials. On October 24, Hitler proclaimed publicly that Poles and Germans would have "to live side by side and get along together."[61]

Marshal Pilsudski now became more amenable to the notion of accord with Germany. On November 15, Lipski met with the führer and explained the marshal's views. Pilsudski saw German withdrawal from the League as an obstacle to Polish security, which was predicated in part on the cooperation between nations through that organization. The marshal would be willing to consider, Lipski conveyed, some form of direct discussions between their two countries. Hitler apparently seized upon the opening and instructed Neurath to draw up the necessary papers.[62] As Hitler allegedly told Dirksen months before, Pilsudski was the only man who could enable German-Polish understanding. Now that the marshal appeared agreeable, Hitler wasted no time.

Throughout November and December, the conditions of a nonaggression pact were ironed out. On November 16, the chancellor authorized the

Foreign Ministry to begin preparing a declaration renouncing the use of war between Germany and Poland. This declaration implied Germany's acceptance of her eastern borders. Neurath continued to make the necessary arrangements and assigned the knowledgeable ministry legal expert, Friedrich Gaus, to work out the finer details. With a Polish-German accord appearing likely, Hitler felt he had removed the possibility of a Polish preventive attack and was thus emboldened to initiate sweeping changes in German troop strength, in stark violation of the Versailles terms. German forces now began planning for a twenty-one division, 300,000-man peacetime army based on one-year service to be ready within four years.[63]

By January 9, Lipski had submitted a revised draft to Neurath and announced Poland's readiness to sign. The German-Polish Declaration of Non-Aggression was signed in Berlin on January 26, 1934. Stating that it would remain in force for at least ten years with the possibility of renewal, the agreement read in part:

> The Polish Government and the German Government consider that the time has come to introduce a new phase in the relations between Germany and Poland by a direct understanding between State and State. . . . Both Governments announce their intention to settle directly all questions of whatever nature which concern their mutual relations.[64]

With these words, the already weakened League suffered another blow to its founding principle of collective security. The German-Polish agreement changed the traditional system of Eastern European alliances since the end of World War I.

Hitler knew that he was buying time with the Polish agreement, and probably so did many of those around him. He even allegedly told Rauschning in early 1934 that the agreement would have "a purely temporary significance. I have no intention of maintaining a serious friendship."[65]

On December 4, 1933, as the details of the Polish pact were being finalized, Hitler's trusted state secretary, Hans Heinrich Lammers, had drafted an urgent and highly sensitive decree at the führer's behest. Various ministries had been using the need to prepare for war to justify their requests for budgetary increases, and Hitler ordered this practice to cease at once. "If it were to be learned that Germany was planning a war," Hitler

admonished, "this could have highly damaging political consequences."[66]
By December 1933, it must have been apparent to many leading Nazi officials, and perhaps to many in the Foreign Ministry as well, that the question was not whether war would come; the question was merely when.

Hitler used the German-Polish nonaggression pact as a public diplomacy weapon, claiming that it demonstrated Germany's peaceful intentions. But those who had carefully read *Mein Kampf* would have recalled his assertion that "one makes alliances only for fighting. And however remote the clash may be at the moment of concluding a treaty, the plan of a belligerent development is nonetheless its inner motive."[67]

Despite the ostensible peace offensive by Hitler and the German Foreign Ministry, not all were fooled by the meaning of the new arrangements. According to Ambassador Moltke on February 19, 1934, the Soviet ambassador in Warsaw was actively seeking further information about the agreement and expected an eventual joint German-Polish attack on the Soviet Union.[68] Ironically, before such a German attack would come, there would first be a joint German-Soviet attack on the Poles.

Many in Poland were skeptical about the new pact. In an unsigned document on March 23, 1934, possibly by Moltke, the author noted that a Polish parliamentarian had presented him with a copy of an SA song that was drawing considerable attention and causing outrage among many. The song spoke of the "damn Poles" and of recapturing what was perceived as German territory. The text was widely published in the press both in Prague and Warsaw. According to the parliamentarian, the pact with Germany was obviously superficial, and Germany's true intentions were reflected in the verses of the SA marching song.[69]

Most of Hitler's advisers within the Foreign Ministry likely recognized what the chancellor intended for Poland. Their decision to support the realignment of relations reflected both their growing fear of encirclement and the increasingly tense environment under which they had to function. Yet the darkening cloud of violence and intimidation that enveloped Germany throughout 1933 was only a hint of the brutality to come. Hitler's realignment of external relations with Poland and the Soviet Union was soon followed by a realignment of internal relations within the Nazi party. The conflict between Hitler and the SA chief, Ernst Röhm, which climaxed in the bloody "Night of the Long Knives," was to have a profound impact not only upon Hitler's future position but also on the decision makers in the Wilhelmstraße. No longer could the diplomats hope that Gestapo and SS measures would be directed solely at the Communists and Jews, for they soon learned that several of the longest knives had been reserved for them as well.

The Longest Knife

2

Control of information in Hitler's Germany was not simply a means for bureaucrats to get ahead; it could also help keep one alive. This fact became frighteningly clear just eighteen months after Hitler took power.

On June 30, 1934, the German government unleashed a reign of terror in what came to be known as the "Night of the Long Knives." Under the direction of Heinrich Himmler, the Schutzstaffeln (SS) executed without trial an unknown number of Sturmabteilung (SA) members. It targeted the three most recent chancellors, arresting one, sending another fleeing into exile, and murdering the third. It assassinated leading political figures and arrested thousands more, imprisoning some and sending others to concentration camps. From this point onward, state-sponsored violence took hold in Germany and did not cease until the Reich's collapse.

One might expect an episode of state-run genocide to have evoked universal opposition from the German public. Yet parts of German society actually welcomed the purge.[1] Many Germans who had embraced the Third Reich as a restoration of "law and order" had doubts about the SA, which had, in the years after the seizure of power, been responsible for countless acts of physical harassment, beatings, and violence against average citizens. The army, for its part, supported the liquidation, providing transport and assistance to the SS and Gestapo firing squads.[2] Members of the business and financial sectors who had feared an SA-led second revolution were surely relieved, believing that the more radical elements of the Nazi Party had been eliminated. There even occurred a modest re-migration of Jews back into Germany, for they believed that their primary adversaries had been removed from power.[3]

But for those who suffered under the threat of violence, the events of June 30 marked a turning point in their relationship to the state. The German government's abandoning the rule of law shocked the conservative diplomats in the Foreign Ministry, whose lives had been devoted to the study and practice of laws, protocols, and codified agreements. Even those aristocratic diplomats less concerned by the murders of SA men, whom they might have viewed as lower class thugs, were deeply frightened by the murder of their colleagues, men of their own ilk and social status.

The murder and attempted murder of former chancellors could not have gone unnoticed by the diplomatic nobility in the Wilhelmstraße, yet they made virtually no documentary records of how they perceived the affair. This is, of course, not surprising. In such an atmosphere, no one would have been so foolish as to have recorded his opposition to the state, lest a similar fate befall him as befell Chancellor Kurt von Schleicher and the others. The fact that the diplomats did not record the episode of domestic terror in any form suggests that they were genuinely frightened by it, especially since ministry officials tended to keep detailed written records.[4] There was very little that these men would not commit to paper and attempt to preserve — except, possibly, for those things deemed too risky or incriminating.[5] Given the intense violence surrounding the SA and SS, the diplomats had good reason to fear for their lives.

The SA, or "Brown Shirts," had played a major part in Hitler's rise to power. They served as a paramilitary band devoted to the Nazi revolution and had been instrumental in the years of struggle against Weimar democracy and against the Social Democratic and Communist forces. They served simultaneously as bodyguards for Nazi leaders and as hecklers who jeered at Hitler's opponents during political rallies. Beyond jeering, they were responsible for countless acts of violence upon those deemed enemies of the Party.

After the Nazis seized power, the SA became more of a liability than an asset. Ernst Rohm, the SA's chief, increasingly showed disrespect toward Hitler, who posed a challenge to his popularity and leadership. Constant

SA assaults were preventing Hitler from gaining broad popular support.

As the months passed for the new regime, Hitler gradually realized that "a controlled and targeted terror could achieve far better results than a continuous orgy of violence."[6]

Rivalries also existed between the SA and the army. Röhm envisioned a vast German army that he would control or in which he would have a leading position. Although his independent militia of nearly two and a half million men dwarfed the German army in size, its members were undisciplined and untested in battle. They obtained substantial Party funds but had little purpose once Hitler came to power. As SA tactics grew increasingly aggressive and uncontrollable, army leaders found civil order at risk. After January 1933, the SA occupied itself with training as a paramilitary force and by conducting numerous parades as a public demonstration of National Socialism's strength. Nonetheless, the tension between the Reichswehr and SA did not recede. On September 1, 1933, Wehrkreis VII in Munich expressed its concern over the large numbers of men who had been dishonorably discharged from the army but who now occupied high positions in the SA. On September 19, attempting to show his support of Nazi Party principles and possibly to ease tension, Blomberg ordered all soldiers to use the Nazi salute when meeting SA members. A month later Lt. Lindwurm of Infantry Regiment 15 was struck in the face by SA men for not saluting an SA flag in Giessen. Blomberg responded by ordering Lindwurm confined to three days' room-arrest.[7]

Foreigners as well suffered from SA assaults. Ivone Kirkpatrick, who served in the British Embassy in Berlin from 1933 through 1936, spent much of his time in the early months "trying to obtain satisfaction for British subjects who had been wantonly assaulted by the SA." One of his staff members was even "attacked in the street for failing to salute an insignificant body marching down Unter den Linden."[8] On another occasion, the SA beat a man for sitting in his car and not saluting the passing of an "old guard" procession in Hamburg. That man, who had to be hospitalized, turned out to be the Portuguese consul-general.[9]

On December 1, 1933, the situation worsened for the Reichswehr when Röhm obtained a cabinet seat. Still keen to demonstrate his support for the Nazi Party, Blomberg ordered in February that soldiers were to wear the Party emblem on their uniforms. But Blomberg's support for the SA was about to evaporate. During a conference of Wehrkreis commanders called by Blomberg in February, a letter arrived from Röhm stating: "I regard the Reichswehr now only as a training school for the German people. The conduct of war, and therefore of mobilization as well, in future is the task of the SA."[10] Röhm's hubris, combined with the SA's waxing aggressiveness and agitation for a second revolution, forced Hitler to intervene.

By the month's end, Hitler decided to back the Reichswehr as the sole bearer of arms in the German nation. In a speech delivered to the heads of army and SA forces on February 28, at the army staff officers' annual dinner, Hitler resolved the brewing conflict. He opposed Röhm's plan to form an SA militia, instead declaring his intention to form a people's army out of the Reichswehr and to limit the SA to political tasks.

Following the dinner, Röhm called a conference of his SA leaders and allegedly proclaimed that the new agreement was another Diktat, explaining that since he could no longer follow Hitler, whom he called the ignorant corporal of World War I, he would have to oppose him. Viktor Lutze, Röhm's deputy, then secretly reported Röhm's remarks, first to Hess, and then to Hitler personally.[11] (After Röhm's assassination, Lutze was rewarded by being named the new SA chief.)

General Reichenau now placed confidence men in the Ausbildungswesen and obtained reports on all phases of SA activities. He even conferred with Himmler on several occasions.[12] Toward the end of June, Sepp Dietrich of the SS met with General Ludwig Beck and informed him that Beck's name was at the top of a list of conservative senior officers whom the SA intended to shoot in a coup d'état. Whether Himmler's SS had actually discovered the SA's true intentions, or whether they merely fabricated the SA hit list in order to gain army backing for the coming purge, may never be known. One thing is clear: General Beck took Dietrich's information seriously enough to have the army headquarters' entire block guarded and to instruct senior officers to keep guns at arm's reach at all times.[13]

By the summer of 1934, German conservatives were living under the looming threat of another revolution. They faced the frequent news of SA attacks on German citizens, soldiers, and foreigners. And they had to face these dangers while under SS and Gestapo surveillance as the wave of state control spread over the nation. The crackdown on Social Democrats, Communists, and trade unionists represented merely the political dimension of state control. Bugging of homes, internal spying, and censorship of the once-free press all increased dramatically, and individual liberty markedly declined. To growing numbers of Germans who suffered under state surveillance, it was becoming apparent by 1934 that the Third Reich had not produced the kind of nation of which they had dreamed. It was within such a climate that the government's highest-ranking conservative at last spoke out.

Matters came to a head on June 17, when Deputy Reich Chancellor Franz von Papen delivered a bold attack on the excesses of Nazi rule. A conservative and recent German chancellor, Papen had acquiesced in forming a government with Hitler at its head in the mistaken belief that Hitler and the Nazis could be contained if surrounded by the moderating influence of conservatives. As this proved impossible, Papen and like-minded politicians grew increasingly anxious. Papen's plan was to gain Hindenburg's support and deliver a withering campaign against Nazi restrictions on personal freedom. He intended to deliver a public address that would clarify the conservatives' views and demonstrate army backing. He hoped to have copies of his speech widely circulated within Germany through his own newspaper agency, Germania Press, to see it covered in the foreign presses, and to record it on gramophone and have it further distributed.[14]

In his public speech at the University of Marburg, Papen warned of the dangers of a second revolution, saying that a nation in permanent revolution could never grow. He criticized the development of a personality cult and openly attacked Goebbels. "Great men," Papen asserted, "are not made by propaganda, but grow out of their actions."[15] The deputy chancellor called for a return to personal freedoms and a free press, and he intimated that the army was behind him. Papen's speech was loudly applauded, and despite Goebbels' ever tightening grip on the German press, the *Frankfurter Zeitung* and some foreign presses published excerpts of Papen's remarks.

One week later, at the German Derby in Hamburg, Papen and Goebbels found themselves together in the grandstand of spectators. Papen received a tumultuous ovation from the crowd, while Goebbels attracted little attention. Observers believed he was furious over Papen's popularity.[16] Papen's speech had struck a chord with many Germans who objected to the expanding state control.

Despite whatever public support he may have enjoyed, Papen's plan backfired, for he had not reckoned on Hitler's willingness to employ violent means. Papen's speech infuriated Hitler and hastened the bloody reprisals.[17]

At the Party rally in Gera that same day, Hitler called Papen's supporters "dwarves" and referred to Papen as a "tiny worm." Hitler continued:

> If they should at any time attempt, even in a small way, to move from their criticism to a new act of perjury, they can be sure that what confronts them today is not the cowardly and corrupt bourgeoisie of 1918 but the fist of the entire people. It is the fist of the nation that is clenched and will smash down anyone who dares to undertake even the slightest attempt at sabotage.[18]

Papen was outraged at Goebbels' censorship of his speech in the press as a whole. On June 20, the deputy chancellor, along with two of his conservative colleagues, Neurath and Finance Minister Lutz Schwerin von Krosigk, went to see Hitler to protest Goebbels' actions and threaten their resignations. Contrary to his remarks a few days earlier, Hitler cleverly told them that Goebbels had not behaved properly and assured them that the SA would be dealt with. Instead of taking a decisive step at that moment, Hitler bought himself time by explaining to them that he intended to discuss the matter carefully with President von Hindenburg very soon.

Although Hitler traveled to Schloß Neudeck for an audience with the ailing president, he was met instead by War Minister von Blomberg. The general informed Hitler that the president was deeply concerned by the SA's agitation and the risk of civil strife. If the chancellor did not take swift and decisive steps, Blomberg insisted, the president would be compelled to declare martial law and place control of the nation in the Reichswehr's hands. Hitler had no intention of allowing power to slip through his fingers. He understood that the crisis demanded action and grasped Blomberg's thinly veiled threat: the price for the army's support was a settlement of the SA question. Papen had clearly miscalculated; Hindenburg was no longer in control. It was von Blomberg and the Reichswehr who, for the moment, held the key to Germany's transition after the president's imminent death.

Forced to choose between the army and the SA as a base of support, Hitler determined to solve the problem by dramatic means. On June 25, General Werner von Fritsch placed army units throughout the country on a state of alert. Three days later the army officially expelled Röhm from membership in the German Officers' League and from all veterans' associations. The following day General von Blomberg pledged the army's full support of Hitler in an article published in the Party's official newspaper, the *Völkischer Beobachter*. If the army had not known of Hitler's intentions, there would have been no need to take these steps at this time.

The most immediate cause of Hitler's decision appears to be the information he obtained from Himmler on June 28. At the wedding of Gauleiter Terboven in Essen, the chancellor received a message from Himmler informing him that Oskar von Hindenburg (the president's son) had agreed to arrange for the president to receive von Papen, probably on June 30. Hitler grasped that Hindenburg's interference, under Papen's influence, could limit his power at a critical juncture.[19]

On the morning of June 30, Hitler traveled to Bad Wiessee, where he arrested Röhm and his cohorts.[20] Goebbels then telephoned Göring in Berlin with the codeword "kolibri" (hummingbird), the signal to set the SS death squads in motion. On July 1, after some hesitation, Hitler decided to have Röhm killed, but he preferred that his old colleague take his own life. Röhm probably viewed suicide as an admission of guilt, and, when he refused to use the pistol left in his cell, an SS guard shot him dead.

These events appear to have shaken even Hitler. For several days after the purge, he seemed nervous and tolerated only the company of his deputy in the Party, Rudolf Hess. Hess assumed a number of Hitler's responsibilities during these days, including meeting with the wife of an SA leader who had been murdered by mistake. The deputy führer also made the first nationwide broadcast explaining what had occurred. Following several tense days, Hitler left Berlin for a vacation with the Goebbels family.[21]

Göring is in part responsible for the dearth of records regarding the purge victims, since he instructed his police to burn all files connected with the affair. Nonetheless, a list named the eighty-five known dead, only fifty of whom were actually SA members. The fact that more than forty percent of those eliminated during the terror had nothing to do with the SA—and therefore with a putsch—is significant. Friends and relatives of those slaughtered had to realize that the putsch scare had afforded the SS and Gestapo with a pretext for indiscriminate murder. At least to some Germans, it had to be apparent that their fates now rested upon an element of caprice.

The official government report placed the death toll at seventy-seven, but some estimates range as high as 150 to 200.[22] Göring's police incarcerated a total of 1,124 people in connection with the episode, and not all their fates are known. For every individual arrested, there were spouses, children, parents, and relatives, friends, acquaintances, and co-workers, all of whom were compelled to wonder why that person disappeared, what became of him, and what it could mean for their own safety.[23]

Once Hitler unleashed the terror of June 30, the long knives cut well beyond Röhm and the SA leadership. Hitler's henchmen struck to eliminate rivals, to settle old scores, and, above all, to leave their mark. The once would-be leader of the Nazi Party, Gregor Strasser, was first kidnapped and then murdered. Former chancellor and Reichswehr general Kurt von Schleicher was murdered in his home. His wife, Elisabeth, who rushed to aid him, was shot to death before the eyes of their young daughter. Chancellor von Schleicher's close colleague and friend, General von Bredow, learned of Schleicher's murder, yet refused to take precautions and was gunned down at home in similar fashion. Aristocrats such as Freiherr von Guttenberg and senior state official Hans Ritter von Kahr suffered the same fate.

Another long knife was pointedly reserved for deputy chancellor von Papen, whose hostile speech had partly triggered this reaction. Papen was arrested in his office and removed from the room under armed guard. He was not murdered; rather, his two top staff members, Herbert von Bose and Edgar Jung, were shot to death: von Bose was assassinated in the vice chancellery; Jung was removed and killed later. No one knows precisely how Jung, known by Goebbels to be the author of Papen's provocative speech, was killed. Goebbels had made a point of noting this in his diary.[24] It was a speech that had publicly criticized Goebbels and brought him embarrassment at the German Derby.

Although Papen's memoirs contain many inaccuracies and therefore must be used cautiously, they provide a compelling account of his experience during the purge—and they are the only firsthand account of his fate. Papen described the scene as follows:

> I got to the office at nine o'clock, to find that Göring's adjutant, Bodenschatz, had already rung several times asking me to call on Göring immediately. Still without any hint as to what was going on, I hurried over to his home in the garden of the Air Transport Ministry, and I remember being amazed to find that the whole area was full of SS guards armed with machine-guns.

Göring was in his study with Himmler. He told me that Hitler
had had to fly to Munich to put down a revolt headed by Röhm, and
that he himself had been given powers to deal with the insurgents in
the capital. I protested immediately at this, and pointed out that I
was the Chancellor's deputy, in his absence such powers could only
be granted to me. Göring would not hear of this and declined flatly to
delegate his authority. With the police and the air force troops under
his command, he was certainly in the stronger position. I then said
that it was essential to tell the President what was happening, declare a state of emergency, and bring in the Reichswehr to restore law
and order. Again Göring refused.

. . . Our discussion became distinctly heated, and Göring cut it short
by stating that my own safety demanded I should return to my home
immediately and not leave it again without his knowledge. I told him
that I would accept full responsibility for my own safety and was not
prepared to submit to what amounted to arrest. While this was going
on, Himmler kept passing messages to Göring. I did not understand
them at the time, but later realized that they were reports of the occupation of my Vice-Chancellery by the SS and the Gestapo.

. . . In the Vice-Chancellery — and all this had to be pieced together
later — Bose had been shot out of hand, for "offering resistance."
My secretary, Baroness Stotzingen, Savigny, and Hummelsheim
had been arrested and carted off to gaol or concentration camps. . . .
I could not understand the arrest of Hummelsheim, who had never
been a member of our inner circle.

. . . My home was surrounded by an SS detachment armed to the
teeth. The telephone was cut off, and in my reception room I found a
police captain, who had had orders that I was to have no contact with
the outside world and that no one was to be allowed to see me.

. . . I spent the next three days completely alone. I had no idea what
was going on in Berlin or in the country as a whole, and expected to
be arrested and probably shot at any moment. I had no doubt that
Goebbels, Himmler, and Heydrich had made up their minds that it
was time for the Marburg reactionary to be liquidated. As I learnt
later, the only man who stood between me and this fate was Göring.

He probably felt that my liquidation would only complicate matters still more.

. . . During these three days I had one tenuous link with the outside world. Certain good friends managed to walk past my windows to convince themselves that I was still alive. One of these was the American Ambassador, Mr. [William E.] Dodd, and another a courageous and well-known medical consultant, Prof. Munk, who refused flatly to be turned away by the guard until he had received a note in my own handwriting proving that I was still alive.[25]

Beyond being harrowing, this experience must have been a bitter pill for the deputy chancellor to swallow, as he had only two weeks earlier proclaimed in his Marburg address: "It would be reprehensible to believe that a people could be unified through terror. The government will counter such attempts because it knows that terror results from a bad conscience, which is about the worst adviser a government can allow itself to have."[26]

Why was Papen spared? After all, it was he who delivered a stirring attack on Nazi rule. It was he who publicly criticized Goebbels, and Goebbels knew it and had helped orchestrate the purge. It was Papen who had protested to Hitler over the ban on his speech. And it was Papen who was set to see Hindenburg to gain his support. It was well known that Papen held considerable influence over the president—the one man who could immediately limit, or even usurp, Hitler's power.

The decision to isolate Papen for three days under house arrest, away from his wife and daughter, but to murder his staff members, was designed to deliver a clear message to Papen and other conservatives in the government: the state possesses both the power and the will to eliminate those who step out of line. Leaving him alive to tell of his experience produced a far greater impact. If the Nazi leaders had merely wanted to prevent him from seeing Hindenburg, then house arrest would have sufficed. Murdering his colleagues, sending the others to concentration camps and jail, occupying his vice chancellery, ransacking its files, and abrogating his authority, all underscored to Papen his complete powerlessness. This message was one that neither Papen nor other like-minded conservatives could fail to understand. The deputy chancellor was released from house arrest and resumed his service in Hitler's regime, but he never again publicly criticized the government or any Nazi leader.

The explosion of terror took its toll on the foreign minister as well. In a meeting with Neurath a few days after the killings, American ambassador Dodd asked Neurath directly what he thought of the affair. Neurath reiterated the standard government line: that Röhm and SA leaders had plotted a putsch and were discovered by the führer. But Dodd's impression was that Neurath was more than uneasy about the situation. He had good reason to be, since his own ministry may also have come under attack.[27]

Early one morning as the purges continued, Gunnar Hagglof, the Swedish envoy in Berlin, was awakened by a frantic phone call. When Hagglof was serving at the Swedish embassy in Moscow in the early 1930s, he had almost daily contact with his German counterparts. One of those was a mid-level German official named Karl Georg Pfleiderer, who had then been a Nazi enthusiast. Pfleiderer refused to give his name over the phone. He said only that Hagglof must meet him at the Zoological Gardens.

Pfleiderer now appeared as a wholly different man from the one Hagglof had known in Moscow. He had gone into hiding at a friend's apartment, his clothes were unpressed, his face unshaven, and he looked around nervously as they spoke. Pfleiderer confessed that his initial enthusiasm for the Nazis had been misplaced. He said that the Nazis' "first duty was to liquidate Marxists and Jews." He reported that masses of people had been arrested without any legal judgment. Hagglof described his friend's change of heart as follows:

> For a long time Karl Georg had tried to tell himself that all these excesses were difficult to avoid in the beginning of a revolution and that the leaders of the movement would soon restore order and discipline. . . . The Night of the Long Knives had killed all his illusions. This time it was not a question of excesses committed by an SA Group or small Party officials. It was the Führer himself who had ordered the bloodbath, the campaign of terror and innumerable arrests. Karl Georg had himself seen the SS police arrest two officials in the Foreign Ministry.[28]

Hagglof further explained that when a friend informed Pfleiderer that his own name appeared on a list of those to be arrested, he sought Neurath's aid. "Neurath said that for the moment he was powerless. He advised Karl Georg to keep away from the Foreign Ministry until further notice." Hagglof advised his friend to come to Sweden for a rest but Pfleiderer expected that he would be arrested at the frontier. He said, "The only thing to do was to wait until von Neurath was able to settle the matter with the Nazi Party."[29] Pfleiderer eventually returned to the ministry and continued to serve the Reich government. Nine years after the purge, as part of the German legation to Stockholm, he again contacted Hagglof and introduced him to Adam von Trott zu Solz, a leader of the German underground resistance movement.[30]

Hagglof's account helps to explain how some conservatives could continue to work for a government that had committed what they viewed as appalling acts of murder and lawlessness. The sense of fear that pervaded Berlin undoubtedly led some individuals to silence their objections and remain obedient. The foreign minister had to witness his subordinates being arrested, while others were forced into hiding and feared for their lives — and Neurath was powerless to stop it.

One conservative who narrowly survived the purges was Bella Fromm. "Frau Bella," as she was known to colleagues and friends, was a highly informed journalist, close to many leading conservatives in the government and the army. An aristocrat who lost her fortune in the inflation years, Fromm worked as a journalist for the *Vossische Zeitung*, writing a daily column on diplomatic life in Berlin. She escaped to America in 1940, and her diary was published two years later with the aid of a former acquaintance, the European desk chief for the *New York Times*. Her diary entries during the purge offer an additional perspective on how conservatives reacted to the affair.

Attending a gala banquet on the evening of July 1, 1934, Bella Fromm noted the following:

> I was greeted by Dr. Sahm [the former mayor of Berlin]. He said, "Thank goodness you are here, Bella." I knew exactly what he thought although he was no longer able to speak frankly, for he was watched day and night. . . . At this point Admiral Raeder arrived. He greeted both of us in the same revealing way. He seemed very uneasy. . . . The party was sheer torture for the German guests; a thrill for the foreigners. We Germans greeted every newcomer with a sigh of relief. Nobody knew who had been lucky enough to escape and who had succumbed. . . . After dinner, when we were grouped in the orangery, a young gentleman of the Wilhelmstraße appeared.

He whispered something into Sahm's ear. Sahm grinned: "Every single one is welcome to me."[31]

Aware that she might be in danger, Fromm spent several days away from the city. Only two weeks earlier she had had General von Schleicher and his wife, along with General von Bredow, to her home for dinner. All three were murdered, and it was known that she was close to them. A few days after the purge, she discovered that her telephone was being tapped and her calls monitored. "Up till now I had refused to believe it when people told me about the Gestapo's listening in."[32]

On July 8, Fromm recorded that a young photographer in her office who was a member of the SS returned to work, having been absent since the day of the purge:

Finally, this morning, he came in—a changed man. He was jittery and uneasy and was constantly watching the door. When questioned as to his strange behavior, he broke into tears and stammered: "I had to shoot in the Gestapo cellar. 37 times I shot. 37 are dead. 37 are haunting me. I can't escape from those 37 ghosts." We were shocked. The "long one," as we nicknamed him, left the office without a "Heil Hitler."[33]

On July 18, she learned that the photographer himself had been killed.[34]

While the average German citizen may have remained essentially untouched by the Röhm affair, conservatives and non-Nazi officials in the army and Foreign Ministry could no longer escape the Gestapo. If even Bella Fromm's newspaper photographer—himself an SS assassin—could be murdered, then non-Nazi conservatives had to wonder how secure their own lives really were. From this point onward, there could be little question in their minds as to the Nazi regime's true nature. Far from the ineffectual Weimar coalitions, this government possessed highly effective means of persuasion and it was willing to use violence against anyone it deemed in opposition. The "Night of the Long Knives" had to have left a deep scar on the memories of German leaders. Of the many long knives, however, the longest was that which cut away the sense of security derived from the rule of law.

Hitler's finance minister, Schwerin von Krosigk, witnessed the randomness with which the SS committed murder. In one example, a renowned music critic, Dr. Wilhelm Schmidt, had been shot to death instead of a different man with the same name. Although Krosigk did not come from a generation in which men freely expressed their emotions or fears, his impersonal comments are quite powerful.

> The shootings without trials were a great blow to the sense of
> justice. . . . It was not the fact that Röhm and sinister figures like
> Heynes in Silesia were executed that damaged the sense of rule of
> law, as much as the manner in which it was done. . . . On that day,
> the dams that safeguarded the certainty of law were torn apart. From
> then on, everything belonging to the German people, from property
> to person, was defenselessly at the mercy of fanaticism, arbitrary use
> of power, and often even adverse chance.[35]

Even within the army, which assisted with the SS assassinations, a number of conservatives objected to the violence of Hitler's actions. General von Hammerstein, for one, disobeyed official orders from Blomberg and attended von Schleicher's funeral. Hammerstein and roughly thirty other generals sent a petition to the president demanding justice, but to no avail. As for General Beck, he would never again support the regime as he had before.

A palpable sense of terror had enveloped Berlin, one apparent even to foreign observers. The French ambassador, André François-Poncet, noted that the killings of SA members could not have gone unnoticed by ordinary Germans in the capital, because the SS "made many arrests all over Berlin. . . . In the suburbs, in the region of the Lichterfelde Barracks, the firing of the execution squads was heard all day long Sunday."[36]

The British embassy official, Ivone Kirkpatrick, was driving home from work when he witnessed the following:

> Armoured cars were appearing from all directions, whole streets were
> being cordoned off and plain-clothes police were swarming every-
> where. I was unable to find out what was happening. It is perhaps not
> surprising, for I heard afterwards that the Minister for Foreign Af-
> fairs and the Minister of Justice were equally ignorant. . . . In a mo-
> ment the whole picture had been altered; many of the most important
> men in Germany disappeared overnight.[37]

The chaotic sense of chance surrounding the entire episode was not lost on Berliners. Kirkpatrick spoke with an elderly electrician immediately after the purge who remarked: "It's an odd world we live in. If I'd said a word against Röhm yesterday I'd be in a concentration camp. It would be more than my life is worth today to say a word in his favor."[38]

The purge's impact on ordinary Germans even seeped into their dreams. Charlotte Beradt, a German journalist, collected the dreams of many average Germans from all social classes throughout the prewar period. One theme she identified running throughout the dreams for the early years under Nazi rule is that of being listened to, observed, and losing one's private space. One man whom Beradt recorded dreamed that he heard on his radio of a general decree against walls as he watched his study walls disappear. Others repeatedly dreamed of common household objects—lamps, mirrors, cushions, desks, clocks, and even an Easter egg—turning into listening devices, recording all they had said and reiterating it spontaneously. These dreams suggest the growing sense among many Germans that life under Nazism was inextricably linked to an insidious sense of subtle terror, even in the early years. Two such dreams are worth retelling here.

A man of about forty, a legal expert employed in municipal administration, told of his dream in which he was speaking to his brother on the telephone around 8 PM. He first took the precaution of praising Hitler's policies and then confided in his brother that nothing gave him pleasure anymore. Later that evening, in the middle of the night, still part of the dream, the phone rang again and a voice said only, "This is the monitoring office." The man described the scene as follows:

> I knew immediately that my crime lay in what I had said about not finding pleasure in anything and I found myself arguing my case, begging and pleading that this one time I be forgiven—please just don't report anything this one time, don't pass it on, please just forget it. The voice remained absolutely silent and then hung up without saying a word, leaving me in agonizing uncertainty.[39]

A middle-aged housewife related a dream in which an SA man was standing over the Dutch oven in her kitchen. He opened it and a penetrating voice repeated everything the family had said that evening. She later noted that the dream probably resulted from some thoughts she had had the previous day at the dentist's office. She had been speaking about some

rumors and although she did not believe that listening devices were present, she caught herself wondering if a machine in the dentist's office could
have contained a microphone. Beradt analyzed the housewife's dream as
that of "a person in the process of being fashioned by a very elusive and
even today not fully understood form of terrorization, a terrorization con-
sisting not of any constant surveillance over millions of people but rather
of the sheer uncertainty about how complete this surveillance was."[40]

Many Germans were becoming aware of the Reich's intrusive nature already at this early stage, even though they themselves might not have been
directly targeted by police surveillance. It is the sense of uncertainty—of
not knowing how safe one truly was—that was quickly enfusing daily life.

Not everyone responded to the purge in precisely the same way. Some
surely reacted in fear and were cowed into submission. Others, like General
Beck and Pfleiderer, may have been frightened, yet they turned to underground resistance activities while remaining servants of the regime. Some,
like Hammerstein and a handful of generals, as noted, defied the state by
protesting to Hindenburg. Those generals no doubt believed that they had
less to fear since they still held a degree of power. By protesting, they took
a considerable risk, for they could not be certain that Hitler was not prepared to strike deeper into his officer corps to purge the army of all resistance. Still others, like Bella Fromm, could no longer live in a state of terror
and eventually fled. And then there were those who were surely frightened
by events, yet continued to serve the state without protest or resistance.
Men like Papen and Neurath numbered among their ranks.

Whatever their individual reaction, June 30 marked a distinct turning
point for Hitler's advisers. Although a gradual build-up of state control
had been under way since the Nazi seizure of power, the Night of the Long
Knives stripped away all pretences. The SA's brutality could have been rationalized as the excesses of an uncontrollable band of fanatics and thugs.
But the SS and Gestapo slayings and arrests could not be interpreted as
such. These were the large-scale, planned actions of the state, not random
beatings or violent outbursts by drunken SA men. June 30 made clear that
a new force in Germany had solidified its power, one that could not be so
easily explained away.

The Night of the Long Knives did not serve to remove a violent element from the Nazi government. It merely replaced it with another, more
sinister, more invasive system, one that possessed the full backing of the

führer and the resources of the state. Ministry officials now functioned under growing Gestapo surveillance: the wire-tapping and internal spying that had become a matter of course after the purge. And this recognition affected their daily lives.

With the climate of fear and uncertainty that descended upon Germany after June 30, ministry officials had to be intensely mindful of the information they controlled. Failure to obtain information on the führer's intentions could be disastrous. Failure to know of one's rivals' activities could result in being outmaneuvered. Even the disclosing of all one's information could be equally unwise

The diplomats also understood that their fates rested not only on their submission to the state but also on an element of chance. Papen was puzzled by the arrest of his associate, Hummelsheim, who had played no significant role in his opposition to Nazi restrictions on personal freedom. Krosigk was aware that a famed music critic had been murdered merely because the assassins had mistaken him for another man with the same name. Neurath knew that his subordinate, Pfleiderer, had been placed on the SS blacklist, yet Pfleiderer had been a Nazi enthusiast. Others surely learned that an SA leader had been assassinated in error and that Hess had had to explain the mistake to the victim's widow. Accidental executions underscored the growing sense of chaos and caprice that characterized SS and Gestapo rule. All these incidents—and there were likely many more about which we will never know—further whittled away the sense of security the diplomats had enjoyed under Weimar democracy, despite its many foibles. After the purge, Neurath and all other decision makers, especially those who were not Nazis, had to be conscious that more than just their careers could be at risk should they fall from favor.

Neurath, who had been a party to Papen's protest following Goebbels' censorship of the Marburg speech, did not suffer directly from any SS intimidation. Yet after the terror, his risk taking became bolder. He made no direct challenges to Hitler or the Nazi system of government, with all its attendant controls, but he did attempt to retain his influence over the führer by controlling the information arsenal. And in his desperate battle for information control, Neurath helped bring Germany to the brink of war.

Risk
in the
Rhineland

3

On Saturday March 7, 1936, Adolf Hitler marched German troops into the demilitarized zone on the Rhine's left bank and in doing so launched his boldest "Saturday Surprise" to date. Against the more cautious advice of his generals, Hitler risked a war when Germany's military was too weak to repel the French. A French counterattack and victory would have been a major setback for Germany's revisionist aims and a serious defeat for Hitler's young regime. Yet no French countermeasures occurred, no strong Western responses were forthcoming, and Hitler's success raised him to new heights of popularity with the German people.

What led Hitler to take such bold action? Historians have often asserted that Hitler merely sensed Allied weakness. Unlike his generals, who studied French troop strength and counted numbers of divisions on the field, Hitler employed his intuition and instinctively sensed the democracies' reluctance to act. Hitler did indeed possess intuition, but was his instinct the principal factor in his decision to remilitarize the Rhine?

There is no question that Hitler intended from early on to cast off the shackles of Versailles, and the reoccupation of the demilitarized zone represented an essential step in that process. This was a goal shared by most German leaders, but to march troops into the Rhineland before German rearmament had reached parity with France's was almost unanimously considered too risky. One man, however, the German foreign minister, Neurath, consistently urged the chancellor onward. In doing so, he took a considerable risk with his own political career.

Neurath's assurances were based not merely on his own political instincts but on reliable intelligence on French political and military leaders. Trusting his ministry's reports that the French would not retaliate, Neurath felt emboldened to encourage the Rhine coup. Gottfried Aschmann, chief of the Foreign Ministry's Press Division, obtained sensitive information on French political and military attitudes over a German reoccupation of the demilitarized zone. Aschmann was a Foreign Ministry career official upon whom Neurath could rely. He had served as consul general in Geneva from 1923 to 1928, at a time when Germany was a major focus of the League, and in 1933 was promoted to director of the ministry's Press Division.[1] His report of January 10, 1936 to Legation Adviser Gustav Braun von Stumm quickly found its way up the hierarchy until it reached von Neurath. Aschmann learned that the French parliamentarian Montigny, who had a close relationship to Prime Minister Pierre Laval, related the following regarding the remilitarization of the Rhine.

> In Paris one begins to realize that Germany wants to overturn the current status, be it through real concerns or fictitious ones. One no longer sees it as an absolute *casus belli*, as in the recent past, but the politicians believe that a judgement on this matter must come first and foremost from the Army General Staff. There has naturally been discussion over the consequences, but to date no consensus has been reached. One group believes that given the extraordinary advances in military motorization, the entire question is less a matter of practical military significance than of moral value for the German self-image. Another group in the General Staff are of the opinion that a remilitarization could only be accepted if a full reorganization of the border defense system were to take place and above all if the defensive garrisons were promptly improved. As the situation stands today, one is neither ready nor willing unhesitatingly to go to war over the eventuality of a German reoccupation.

This last sentence was underlined, possibly by Neurath. The report continued by noting Montigny's wish for a peaceful resolution through negotiations rather than German military action. Aschmann concluded by citing Montigny as saying, "If it becomes apparent that Germany merely wishes to regain her sovereignty in the Rhineland and wants to refrain from a provocative overmilitarization on France's border regions, then the entire affair need not necessarily result in excessive tension or danger."[2]

With this information in hand, Neurath could argue that France would not fight over German remilitarization. He would also stress the need to limit the number of troops employed so as not to appear immediately hostile. In contrast to the reluctant minister of war, von Blomberg, Neurath could urge that military operations proceed. As for Hitler, he could appear bold, daring, and endowed with an uncanny sense for divining the weakness of his adversaries.

Aschmann's intelligence was not the only information Neurath possessed. Signs of French weakness could be read in the French papers, which revealed a considerable degree of political disunity. The divisive climate led the German ambassador in Paris, Roland Köster, to notify Berlin that in his view the French people would not support a military operation beyond their borders.[3] Reports on French political squabbling and Köster's perception of French public opinion may have further strengthened Neurath's conviction that France would not fight. Neurath also received information on Italy's position regarding France from the German ambassador in Rome, Ulrich von Hassell. Although Hassell's reports proved of great value during the Rhineland crisis, neither his nor Ambassador Köster's assessments provided the foreign minister with the sensitive information found in Aschmann's report, which represented a more detailed analysis of the mood among French political and military leaders.

Despite the obvious significance of Aschmann's report, there is no documentary evidence that Neurath shared this information with Hitler, and there is reason to suspect that he did not. Hitler's actions after January 10, the date of Aschmann's report, suggest that he had no knowledge of it. But why would the foreign minister have withheld such critical information?

Although nearly two years had passed since the Night of the Long Knives, the foreign minister could not feel secure in his position. Even if no further incidents of domestic terror occurred after June 30, 1934, the memory of mass arrests and indiscriminate murder could not have been forgotten. Of course, other forms of state-sponsored intimidation continued, mainly in the form of Gestapo surveillance and wire-tapping led by Göring's Forschungsamt. The memory of June 30 and the awareness of being spied on was sufficient to cause Neurath to adapt his behavior. However, he had to confront a more constant and pressing threat to his security, one that intensified his control of the information arsenal.

From the moment Hitler assumed the chancellorship, Neurath found his authority increasingly challenged from various sides. Nazi Party officials sought in early 1933 to infiltrate the Foreign Ministry with Party members, but Neurath and Bülow were largely successful in resisting such attempts. The Party did manage to gain control over the ministry's Personnel Department, but even this did not significantly affect the key diplomatic positions. Nazi incursions into the ministry's domain, however, remained a trademark of Hitler's regime and a constant stress for Neurath.

On March 19, 1935, both Neurath and Bülow received a memorandum from the ministry's personnel director, Werner Freiherr von Grünau.

In the more than two years since the Machtergreifung, it has not been possible to achieve a relationship of trust between the Foreign Ministry and the Party. There are [examples], however, in some cases, of good relationships such as between Hitler and Neurath. Distrust has come from the removal of some members of the Ministry and from the fact that the Führer's representative is newly controlling personnel matters. Some Ministry officials, although they are now entering the Party, fear for their careers. The Personnel Department has a plan and there will only be a few victims.[4]

Hitler himself, who disliked the conservative élites in the ministry but depended on them, criticized Neurath and his colleagues. On November 4, 1935, Neurath recorded Hitler's censure: "The Foreign Ministry does not cooperate. It remains outside the movement. It does not want to understand the Führer's policies and creates difficulties everywhere."[5]

Neurath confronted not only Hitler's dissatisfaction with the ministry's aversion to the Nazi Party but also faced ongoing battles with the Auslandsorganisation (AO), the Party institution responsible for Germans living abroad. Territorial disputes typified the relationship between these two competing institutions as the AO wrangled with the Foreign Ministry over which organization was responsible for German representatives in foreign lands.[6]

Beyond having to fend off Nazi Party incursions into the ministry's domain, Neurath additionally had to endure the interminable struggle with his principal rival and would-be successor, Joachim von Ribbentrop, who proved a perpetual thorn in Neurath's side. Ribbentrop's adventures in London as the führer's special envoy created confusion and ill-will on all sides.

On July 5, 1934, immediately following the bloody Röhm purge, Bülow reported to Neurath on the results of Ribbentrop's trip. Bülow described his telephone conversation with the German ambassador in London, Leopold von Hoesch, who explained that Ribbentrop had phoned him with three tasks to fulfill. The third of Ribbentrop's demands, however, was so confused that Hoesch could not comply without written instructions. Ribbentrop spoke to Hoesch only in coded language, and Hoesch could make no sense of it. To clarify his instructions, Ribbentrop informed Hoesch that he would send the ambassador a special emissary whose name would begin with the letter "F."[7] No doubt imagining himself a cloak-and-dagger character from a spy novel, Ribbentrop succeeded only in reinforcing the already growing view among diplomats in Germany and abroad that he possessed neither the wit nor the common sense to execute the duties Hitler had assigned him. Neurath promptly wrote to Hitler that Ribbentrop's London adventures had been a "total failure."[8] Despite his diplomatic and social failures with the British upper class, Ribbentrop was not to be so easily discouraged.

As the Rhine crisis mounted in 1935, Neurath found himself still besieged by the intrusive Ribbentrop. Ribbentrop attempted to wheedle his way into Neurath's domain by planting one of his personal representatives—or spies—at the foreign minister's daily top-level meetings. On January 19, 1935, Neurath responded to Ribbentrop's attempt by explaining that he was not invited to participate in the daily morning meetings because they were restricted to a small number of ministry directors. Neurath said that he had no wish to increase the circle of participants and that such was unnecessary in Ribbentrop's case because he already received the same information from the Propaganda Ministry's daily conferences. Neurath added a stinging paragraph to emphasize Ribbentrop's misbehavior.

> I would like at this time to mention that you have not found it necessary recently to inform me of your activities as the Chancellor has directed. I have not yet discussed this with the Chancellor because I am regularly informed by him of internal directives. Nevertheless, I would like to point out that it does correspond to the Chancellor's

will to separate individual aspects of foreign policy from the Foreign Ministry, which I direct. . . . You should inform me of your activities regarding disarmament.[9]

Not until the end of May did Ribbentrop reply, brashly commanding Neurath to inform *him* of Neurath's activities. Ribbentrop concluded his effrontery with a postscript asserting that he would be sending a representative to participate in the morning policy conferences.[10] Two days later, on May 29, the unmistakably vexed foreign minister told Ribbentrop: "Your request to be informed of all Foreign Ministry activities would mean that you would receive copies of all correspondence." Given the volume of cable traffic that passed daily from Berlin to its multifarious divisions, embassies, consulates, and to other government ministries, the ludicrousness of Ribbentrop's request should have been apparent even to him. Neurath pointedly remarked that "in your appointment notice from the previous year it states that you are under my direction. I am not aware of any change in this status. . . . [F]or months I have not received either a verbal or written report of your activities."[11]

Within this climate of perpetual infighting and internecine territorial rivalries between the Foreign Ministry and Party interlopers, Neurath felt compelled to tighten his control over the information flow to Hitler. It was an unstable environment that only worsened as the Rhineland crisis mounted.

The Rhineland crisis stemmed from Articles 42 and 43 of the Versailles treaty by which Germany was forbidden to station troops beyond a fifty-kilometer zone on the Rhine's right bank. The purpose of this restriction was to prevent a German attack on her eastern neighbors by leaving her vulnerable to a French counterattack in the west. The Locarno agreement, signed by Germany, Italy, France, and Great Britain, reaffirmed these restrictions and provided mutual assurance of territorial integrity. If France should attack Germany, Italy and Britain would come to Germany's aid. Thus, the demilitarized zone, defended by the Locarno powers, ensured German and French security, but it also meant that Germany accepted her borders as fixed by the hated Versailles treaty. German revision of that "dictated" peace, a main aim of all German parties across the political spectrum since 1919, was therefore predicated on remilitarizing the Rhineland.

So stood the matter in the years immediately following World War I. A demilitarized Rhineland served as the cornerstone of French security. However, dramatic developments in military technology were to change the situation substantially by the mid-1930s and diminish the Rhineland's strategic value in the eyes of the French general staff. The evolution of airplanes meant that the terrain could be crossed in minutes. Improvements in motorized vehicles—especially in tanks and personnel carriers—seemed to reduce the need for a demilitarized Rhineland still further. Despite these technological advances, a demilitarized zone would have contributed to French security. Nevertheless, by early 1936, the French general staff had essentially written it off as a serious factor.

Paris was wholly incapable, both militarily and financially, of defending the zone. As French policy makers cut military spending substantially, the French military were compelled to economize on research and development of new weapons systems, weapons procurement, and training. Moreover, the commitment to constructing the Maginot Line, made in the prosperous 1920s, limited the army's options during the depression era, since those fortifications had to be brought to completion lest the entire investment have been in vain. It was not the lack of French will to fight in 1936 that permitted Hitler's coup, but rather France's lack of funds, military might, and therefore operational plans to counter a German remilitarization.[12]

Despite France's financial and military deficiencies, the French military was far stronger than German forces in 1936. France's financial woes and technological advances may have encouraged French leaders to perceive the zone as unimportant—and Aschmann's intelligence would tend to corroborate this view. Conversely, the German general staff fully recognized the zone's relevance for any future operations and respected French military superiority.

With the general staff convinced of French superiority, how did Hitler know that the French were unprepared to retaliate? Did Hitler hold his finger to the west wind, hoping to gauge currents drifting out of Paris, or did he possess information that led him to believe in the French army's impotence?

The first trickle of intelligence to reach Berlin regarding French abandonment of the Rhine demilitarized zone came in 1934, as a result of Leon Blum's leak to German officials.[13] More intelligence would arrive later to confirm further French military weakness. Following Hitler's announcement of Germany's return to conscription in March 1935, however, a side show theater of war occupied the führer's attention.

One issue that German leaders needed to follow was Italy's relations with the other Locarno powers. Italy's estrangement from France and

Britain over oil sanctions placed France in a highly vulnerable position.
Reluctant to defend the Rhineland alone, and never able to extract satis-
factory security guarantees from Britain, France had hoped for joint military operations with the Italian army. Knowing French long-term security
interests lay with Britain, whose industrial base and economic strength far
exceeded Italy's, French leaders found themselves in the awkward position
of seeking military cooperation with two incompatible allies. Since Italy
and Britain had clashing interests in the Mediterranean, France could not
ally with one without alienating the other. Mussolini's invasion of Ethiopia
demanded some public show of Western disapproval. With the threatened
imposition of oil sanctions against Italy, the facade of a solid Stresa front
was exposed as hollow.

Some have argued that the Abyssinian conflict, more than any other
factor, led Hitler to launch his coup because it convinced him of Allied disunity.[14] It is true that the German Foreign Ministry received several reports
from Ambassador Hassell in Rome that Mussolini saw the so-called Stresa
front as a dead issue and that Italy would not support France militarily
against Germany. Yet the Abyssinian affair served only to leave France devoid of Italian aid; it did not show French unwillingness to mobilize alone.
There is little documentary evidence from the standard published sources
to indicate that Hitler and Neurath were convinced that France would not
act alone to defend the Rhine. Those documents refer either to reports from
Ambassador von Hassell in Rome regarding Italian officials' impressions
of French weakness, or they refer to reports from German Ambassador
Köster in Paris regarding his belief that the French people would oppose
military action beyond their frontiers. Only one document from the published sources, a report from Köster on November 27, 1935, suggests that
France would not fight without Britain, and this impression was gained
not by Köster directly, but from what Laval allegedly told Sieburg, the
Paris correspondent for the *Frankfurter Zeitung*. One source, however,
suggests that France would fight. Dirk Forster, German chargé d'affaires,
sent a February 7 cable to Berlin recording Flandin saying that in the event
of a flagrant breach, "France would proceed to mobilize."[15]

Others have asserted that Hitler's risk in the Rhineland was prompted
by his need to fuel domestic support for the regime and to distract attention
from unpopular issues such as the church conflict and growing food shortages.[16] The foreign policy success in the Rhine was to be exploited in the
upcoming Reichstag elections with the expectation that a remilitarization

would enhance the Party's reputation and heighten its public approval. But a remilitarization had no guarantee of success. If Germany were forced to withdraw from the zone, domestic support for the Party would have dropped even further. Domestic concerns would have to have been paramount to warrant such a risk. Without reliable information on French intentions, remilitarization had to be a gamble.

The Germans were, of course, not the only ones seeking information on the Rhineland. At the same time that Neurath was obtaining intelligence on French political and military plans, Soviet agents were ascertaining German intentions regarding the Soviet Union and the Rhine. On January 15, 1936, agents of the Soviet security service, the NKVD, produced a top secret report entitled "Summary of Military and Political Intelligence on Germany." Having gained access to American diplomatic circles in Berlin, Soviet agents learned that the German government was conducting a probe to determine the positions of other states in the event of an armed conflict between Germany and the Soviet Union. Whether this alleged German probe represented a low-level government feeler or indicated more serious German intentions is unclear. Regardless of the probe's origin, such reports did little to assuage Soviet concerns over Germany's intentions and no doubt provided a fillip to Stalin's quest for security pacts, be they with the Western powers or with Hitler himself.

Embedded further in the NKVD assessment lay a citation from the Foreign Ministry state secretary. When asked of Germany's position in the event of French and British military collaboration, Bülow allegedly said, "We would view this as a violation of Locarno, and if we are not dragged into participating in negotiations, we will not consider ourselves bound to the Locarno obligations concerning the preservation of the Rhine demilitarized zone."[17]

The NKVD report highlights two important facts. Not only did the British and French have early warnings of remilitarization; American and Soviet officials expected Hitler's move as well. How far the NKVD assessment traveled through the Kremlin hierarchy is uncertain, but it is fair to state that Hitler's so-called "Saturday Surprise" in the Rhine was a surprise to very few. It also indicates that Bülow, as well as Neurath and probably most others in the Foreign Ministry, were anxious to break free of Locarno and thereby terminate Germany's first security accord with Britain since 1871. Nonetheless, it was Neurath, not Bülow, who advocated the early Rhine invasion. Apart from the foreign minister, however, it appears that all the members of Hitler's inner circle opposed a premature deployment of troops.

At this time, Hitler's inner circle consisted of his military leaders, along with Göring, Goebbels, Ribbentrop, and Neurath. Hess and Interior Minister Wilhelm Frick did not count among those closest to the führer during the crisis and were not even notified of the decision to deploy troops until the evening of March 3.[18] There is no question that the German military supported the idea of remilitarization. Control of the railways on both sides of the Rhine was considered essential for the eventual expansion to a thirty-six-division army. Army leaders did urge caution regarding the timing of the move. Generals Blomberg and Fritsch both expressed reservations about the reoccupation in March, and they warned Hitler to be prepared for withdrawal if France retaliated.[19] General Beck, who respected the French army's superiority at this time, also objected to the invasion.[20] While an enthusiastic supporter of remilitarization as part of his plan for the rebuilding of German military might, Beck opposed a premature military action.[21] The generals were all too aware that German forces had only just begun to expand following the return to conscription the previous year and that rearmament was still at an embryonic stage. The reserve of the nation's highest-ranking generals bolstered Neurath's position vis-à-vis the army, making him appear as a bold risk taker, a quality Hitler strongly favored in his advisers.

The generals' reluctance suggests that they were not receiving any military intelligence to indicate French weakness, or they doubtless would have supported the move in March. In fact, what military intelligence the generals did receive seems to have heightened their anxiety. Both military attachés in London and Paris misperceived those governments' likely responses to a German reoccupation, expecting that the British and French would answer with troops or sanctions. For weeks prior to remilitarization, the military attaché in Paris, Kühlenthal, cabled both the War and Foreign ministries that both Britain and France appeared determined to stand firm. On January 9, he reported that Britain allegedly intended to deploy motorized units to support French garrisons in the south should Italy prove hostile.[22]

On February 20, barely two weeks before reoccupation, Kühlenthal sent Berlin a detailed report on the Anglo-French military conversations earlier in the year. The attaché noted that although no military agreements had been finalized, the atmosphere for their conclusion was set and they might occur at any time. Kühlenthal warned: "Therefore, I see a serious danger arising for us if Germany undertakes any action which goes against the current dogma, primarily in the Rhineland zone— especially dangerous west of the Rhine —and in the Anschluss question."[23]

Kühlenthal was not alone in his reservations. Even after the initial German deployment, the attaché in London, Geyr von Schweppenburg, became so unsettled that he disregarded protocol by sending his report directly to War Minister Blomberg, rather than to General Beck. Geyr cabled Blomberg on March 12, saying that the joint opinion of the military, naval, and air attachés in London was that the "situation should be regarded as exceptionally grave."[24] This information may have frazzled Blomberg's nerves so much that he called for a partial withdrawal.[25] It is no wonder that Blomberg and the other generals had misgivings since the information presented to them by their key military attachés strongly indicated French resolve.

Göring's fear of a French counterattack is clear. According to the Polish ambassador in Berlin, Jozef Lipski,

> Göring was visibly terrified by the Chancellor's decision to remilitarize the Rhineland, and he didn't conceal that it was taken against the Reichswehr's advice. I had several talks with him then. I found him in a state of utmost agitation, and this was just at the time of the start of the London Conference. He openly gave me to understand that Hitler had taken this extremely risky step by his own decision, in contradiction to the position taken by the generals. Göring went so far in his declaration as to say literally that, if France entered upon a war with Germany, the Reich would defend itself to the last man, but that, if Poland joined France, the German situation would be catastrophic. In a broken voice Göring said that he saw many misfortunes befalling the German nation, bereaved mothers and wives. . . . Göring's breakdown during the Rhineland period made me wonder about his psychological stamina. I thought this might be due to his physical condition, since he was using narcotics.[26]

Ribbentrop's position on the Rhineland is ambiguous. He favored remilitarization, and he may have, at times, encouraged the chancellor to move in March. However, some documents indicate the opposite. According to one report by Hassell, Ribbentrop revealed himself as needlessly alarmist. On February 19, Hitler summoned Hassell and Neurath to him. Ribbentrop was also present. The führer explained that a correspondent had reported that Mussolini actually held firm to Locarno and Stresa and that they must move with greater caution. Ribbentrop declared that Germany's intentions would be given away to the French. Hassell replied that one should not make too much of such reports and that there was nothing to reveal to the French, since Germany's intentions were already "in the air."[27] (Despite Hassell's soothing words, the führer was evidently not mollified, for on February 22, Hassell related Hitler's displeasure over the correspondent's information to Mussolini personally.)[28] Hassell's report suggests that not only was Ribbentrop ill-informed, he may have been encouraging Hitler's caution. In any case, Ribbentrop's influence at this time does not appear to have been significant.

Goebbels also had reservations about the timing of reoccupation. He advised Hitler to wait until the French Senate had ratified the Franco-Soviet alliance, thereby providing greater justification when presenting Germany's action to the public.[29] On March 1, he referred to the period as a "critical moment" but noted, "He who risks nothing, wins nothing."[30] During these days, Goebbels repeatedly recorded his difficulty sleeping and commented on the nerve-racking atmosphere.[31]

As for the führer himself, he allegedly even remarked to Foreign Ministry interpreter Paul Schmidt: "The 48 hours after the march into the Rhineland were the most nerve-racking in my life. If the French had then marched into the Rhineland we would have had to withdraw cursing and in shame, for the military forces at our disposal would have been wholly inadequate for even a moderate resistance."[32]

The traditional interpretation of Neurath during the Rhineland crisis holds that he exhibited great caution. "Foreign Minister Neurath also had grave doubts. He thought 'speeding up' the action was not worth the risk."[33] This view rests on three secondary sources and one primary source.[34] Each of the three secondary accounts ultimately refers back to the one primary source as evidence. In other words, the traditional interpretation of Neurath's caution during the crisis rests heavily on a single document. Such a source is worthy of careful consideration.

This document is not a report from Neurath expressing his concerns over an early remilitarization. Instead, it is a memorandum from Ambassador von Hassell noting his *impression* of what Neurath believed. Hassell's note on his meetings of February 19 with Neurath, Hitler, and Ribbentrop says that Neurath agreed with Hassell that reoccupation prior to the French senate's ratification of the Franco-Soviet pact was unnecessary and unwise. Hassell recorded: "Neurath does not believe that they will march against us, but we cannot merely think about the moment. The consequence will be a general concentration against us. We are already isolated enough."[35]

Thus, the notion that Neurath harbored "grave doubts" actually hinges on two assumptions: first, that Hassell accurately assessed Neurath's true convictions, and second, that Neurath revealed to Hassell his true convictions. Hassell may have projected his own caution onto Neurath, believing him to be a like-minded conservative.[36] However, Neurath understood the value of information control, and if he had indeed been urging the chancellor onward, then he would have had no incentive to reveal this fact to the ambassador. It was to the foreign minister's advantage that he appear to be of similar mind to Hassell, for he needed the ambassador's assistance in garnering information.

Hassell also noted in his memorandum that in Hitler's presence the foreign minister seemed to silence his objections and accept Hitler's stand. Taken at face value, the document suggests Neurath's caution or subservience. But read in the context of the uncertain environment in which Neurath had to function, the document can be interpreted quite differently. Viewed in this light, it suggests that Neurath did not silence his objections, but rather that he had none. From this vantage point, it is not surprising that the same document records Hassell's confusion over the foreign minister's behavior. Hassell noted that on the morning following these discussions, immediately prior to boarding the train for Rome, he sought out General Fritsch and voiced his concerns. Hassell told Fritsch that although Neurath had expressed grave doubts to him, the foreign minister had refused to make plain his objections to the führer. Given Neurath's position, it is entirely feasible that he was presenting one face to Hassell and a quite different one to Hitler.

Paul Schmidt, the chief interpreter in the Foreign Ministry, testified at the Nuremberg war crimes trial that Neurath was the sole individual in the Wilhelmstraße who assured Hitler of French weakness.[37] When the prosecution confronted Neurath with Schmidt's testimony, the foreign minister denied having known of Hitler's plans to remilitarize the Rhineland until one week before the führer made his decision. Published German Foreign Ministry records prove that Neurath knew well of Hitler's plans at least three months earlier, and probably well before then. In a meeting on December 14, 1935 between Hitler, Neurath, and the British Ambassador Eric Phipps, Neurath essentially told the ambassador that Germany would remilitarize the Rhineland if the present circumstances continued unchanged.[38]

Searching for security through multilateral agreements, the British hoped throughout 1935 to entreat Germany to sign an air power pact limiting Germany's first-strike capability and presumably enabling inspection of German air bases and arms. Hitler argued at length that Germany could not enter into further multilateral accords when they had clearly proved worthless, pointing to the recent Franco-Soviet alliance as evidence that the Locarno agreement was now dead. In the event of a Soviet attack on Poland, Hitler argued, Germany could not sit idly by, but would be compelled to stand with Poland. France, in accordance with her new bilateral military alliance, would support the Soviets by entering the Rhineland to draw German troops westward. Hitler thus used the Franco-Soviet alliance as a justification for the Rhineland's remilitarization. He added that if the British signed an air power pact with France, Britain, too, would be allied against Germany.

Phipps responded by asserting that it would be wiser to reduce the Soviet danger by including the Soviets in the European system, rather than by forming a collective front against them. Hitler's rejoinder was typical of his anti-Communist rhetoric: "This is like believing that one can close a virus in a closet for a time, only later to release it, believing it then less dangerous." Phipps could have pointed out to the führer that throughout the 1920s, Germany had engaged in a close military alliance with the Soviet Union for the training of German soldiers, the production of poison gas and Junker airplanes, all on Russian soil, in violation of the Versailles treaty.

As Neurath noted in a memorandum summarizing the meeting, he concluded the discussion by pointing out to Phipps that "a relocation of the British air force bases closer to the Franco-Belgian borders would result in our moving our air force closer to those borders as well, beyond the fifty-kilometer zone where they stand at present. This must be done to avoid the potential destruction of our industrial area." To underline his point and leave no room for misinterpretation, Neurath said, "This would, in that event, mean the end of the demilitarized zone."[39] Britain was thus forewarned.

Neurath pursued a policy of deception toward the British over Germany's air power. None in the German leadership had any intention of sharing accurate information about the Luftwaffe's true strength. Neurath noted that Hitler at this meeting offered to share information on German air power with the British government, provided it were reciprocal and remained secret. The two nations later agreed to an exchange of air attachés for the purpose of mutual inspection of air forces. The foreign minister recorded that "although the English air attaché will be well treated by our military people, he will learn far less of the German air disarmament and airplane industry than will his German counterpart in England."[40] Deception and espionage played a principal role in German revisionist aims, and Neurath showed no hesitation to employ these means, for he fully recognized the value of intelligence.

At the Nuremberg trial, when the prosecution questioned Neurath about how he knew that the French would not retaliate, the defendant answered merely that he was convinced based on his understanding of the international situation.[41] Neurath's decision to urge Hitler onward was based neither solely on political acumen nor on raw instinct but also on the intelligence gained from his Foreign Ministry colleagues.

Did Neurath, in possession of vital intelligence from Aschmann as of January 10, share this information with the führer or instead choose to keep it from him? If Neurath did in fact pass on Aschmann's intelligence, then the notion that Hitler acted predominantly on instinct during the crisis must be modified. If, on the other hand, Neurath elected not to reveal his inside information to the führer, then our understanding of Neurath during the crisis must be altered. Based on the chancellor's behavior, it appears that he had no specific knowledge of French military weakness.

In a meeting on February 12 with Neurath, Ribbentrop, Blomberg, and Dirk Forster, Hitler interrogated the latter on his views regarding the likely French responses to remilitarization. Hitler asked pointedly if Forster could guarantee the success of the impending move, to which Forster replied in the negative. According to Forster's account, Hitler was agitated, sarcastic, and deeply concerned about French retaliation.[42]

Two days later, on February 14, the German ambassador in Rome, Ulrich von Hassell, reported that the führer was still considering whether to remilitarize the Rhineland and was seeking to learn Mussolini's reaction.[43] Hitler appeared cautious, aware that a military defeat at French hands could prove ruinous for his future plans.

Goebbels observed Hitler's uncertainty. On several occasions in the days preceding the deployment of troops, Goebbels noted that Hitler's mood was somber and that the decision before him was difficult. On February 28, and again on March 1, he remarked that Hitler had still not reached a decision.[44]

The question remains whether and why Neurath may have withheld Aschmann's intelligence from the führer when so much was at stake for Germany. The prestige and power of the German foreign minister — the pinnacle position in the bureaucracy's hierarchy — brought with it a simultaneous decrease in security. In the Nazi dictatorship's perilous atmosphere, the foreign minister's position became all the more unstable. In the event of a diplomatic defeat, Hitler would never have resigned the chancellorship, and Neurath would have been held responsible. Since the Night of the Long Knives, Neurath had to remain deeply concerned over his delicate position. The Rhineland crisis brought all such dangers to the fore.[45]

Once Neurath obtained Aschmann's intelligence that the French general staff would not fight over the demilitarized zone, the foreign minister confronted a critical choice. If advocating remilitarization turned out to be in error and the French should retaliate, it would not matter where or how Neurath obtained his convictions over French weakness. Hitler would surely have made him a scapegoat for the disaster. Even if Hitler were to prove forgiving, a military, and therefore political, defeat in the Rhineland would have substantially diminished Neurath's credibility and hastened his dismissal. On the other hand, if Aschmann's intelligence proved accurate and no French attack ensued, then by advocating remilitarization without revealing his sources, Neurath would appear prescient and endowed with keen political insight, enhancing his job security in a highly uncertain climate.

The tense, uncertain position of being a chief bureaucrat within Hitler's dictatorship led Neurath to circumvent standard operating procedures. Under siege from hostile Nazi Party elements attempting to whittle away his authority and dominion over foreign policy, Neurath had to defend himself by whatever means necessary. He learned to guard what information he could obtain and to turn it to his advantage whenever possible. To that end, the foreign minister had to gain access to information ahead of Ribbentrop and control its flow to the führer. Fortunately for Neurath, he had assistance.

Ulrich von Hassell, a conservative diplomat of the "old school," assisted Neurath in his efforts to ascertain the führer's will. On January 20, 1936, Hassell cabled the foreign minister with a lengthy memorandum. By way of conclusion, Hassell explained that Italian Ambassador Bernardo Attolico was concerned about Germany's proposed re-entry into the League just as Italy was preparing to leave it. Hitler's public allusions to a possible German re-entry, however, were never made in earnest. Hassell related that Hitler told him that he had no intention of rejoining the League, precisely the kind of information Neurath needed.[46] It was by no means surprising that Hitler should have shared some of his intentions with Hassell, since the führer relied heavily in the early years on his diplomats, and especially on Hassell, for cables on the situation in foreign capitals.[47]

On February 14, 1936, Hassell officially cabled the Foreign Ministry to detail his discussions with Hitler regarding Italy and remilitarization.[48] Hassell reported that Hitler was considering whether he should use the Franco-Soviet Pact as a pretext for remilitarizing the Rhineland but wanted first to obtain Hassell's insights on Italy's position. Although Hitler believed the Western powers to be disunited and unlikely to respond militarily, he was concerned about gaining Mussolini's consent before German troops marched. Clearly, the chancellor was uncertain and cautious. Hitler's sole direct reference to France suggested his belief that she was distracted by domestic political events. From Hassell's account, it is evident that Hitler had not yet firmly decided to take the step Neurath had been advocating.

According to the printed sources, *Documents on German Foreign Policy*, no other record of these talks has been found. It has therefore been assumed that Hassell's meeting with the führer occurred on February 14, as his official cable indicated. But Hassell's discussions with the führer had to have occurred earlier, for contained within Neurath's files are Hassell's original, handwritten notes on his conversation with the führer, but the dates of this draft and his official cable to the Foreign Ministry do not coincide. Hassell's original notes are dated "Beginning of February 1936," whereas the official, revised version is dated February 14.

Why would Hassell have sent the German foreign minister his hand-written notes of discussions with Hitler, only to send essentially the same report through official channels a week or two later? Seen in the context of intragovernmental political infighting, the answer is clear. Neurath needed to obtain information on Hitler's thinking ahead of his rivals, principally Ribbentrop, and Hassell was all too willing to aid the foreign minister in his efforts to defend the ministry from the Party's growing incursions.

On March 5, Hitler set the date of March 7 for the deployment of troops. Even as German forces were entering the zone, Hitler announced the action while making sweeping peace offers to the French. The chancellor proposed a twenty-five-year nonaggression pact with both France and Belgium, to be guaranteed by Britain and Italy. For Britain, he raised the hope of Germany's signing an air power pact, and he spoke of forming nonaggression pacts with Germany's eastern neighbors along the lines of the German-Polish agreement.[49] He even suggested that Germany might re-enter the League. All these proposals were designed in part to defuse French public support for retaliation and to enable Hitler to present himself as a man of peace — an important element in the image he strove to create for the German populace. In addition to making grandiose peace overtures, Hitler hoped to reduce the risk of a French attack by sending only 3,000 of the 30,000 troops deep into the zone. Additional troops were disguised to appear as SA and Labor Front members on training exercises.[50] If Hitler had not feared a French response, such measures would not have been necessary.

To Hitler's and his advisers' relief, and to the German people's jubilation, there was no danger after all. As Neurath had predicted, no French retaliation accompanied German remilitarization and Hitler had his coup. A flutter from the French and bluffs to mobilize shook Blomberg's nerves and led him to propose a partial withdrawal of German forces. Neurath, not fearing a French reprisal, held firm. His steadiness of nerve impressed the chancellor and, for the moment at least, he had outshone his rivals.[51]

Despite Neurath's elevated status in Hitler's eyes, the foreign minister knew that his position was by no means secure. Although his gamble of consistently encouraging remilitarization had paid off, he still sought to maximize the profits it had yielded. In a written criticism of Blomberg's policies shortly after the crisis subsided, Neurath attempted to show the führer that his own insights were superior to those of the war minister. On March 27, Blomberg sent Neurath the military's contribution on remilitarization to be included in a statement to the English government. Blomberg contended that no permanent fortifications would be built before September 30 at the earliest—a markedly conciliatory tone. Only if France and Belgium acted in a manner that necessitated it would Germany build permanent field fortifications. If England wished a mutual assistance pact, then the military was prepared to grant it.[52] Laying out the failings embedded in Blomberg's stance, Neurath set forth his own plans to avoid committing Germany to any settlement that could result in making the present territorial boundaries fixed and permanent.

> We must guard ourselves against strengthening the impression (from this or other such acts) that France and Belgium are threatened by us, as if they had a claim to compensation for the decrease in their security. We dare not admit that a dangerous situation exists on the western border. This would lead the Locarno powers to press their absurd demands for a transitional government.[53]

In order to elevate further the Foreign Ministry over the War Ministry regarding foreign policy, Neurath made certain to send Hitler copies of Blomberg's letter along with his reply.[54] Despite his extraordinary triumph in the Rhine, he felt compelled to continue his ongoing battle for the führer's favor.

As for Hitler, his risk in the Rhineland proved a public relations coup. His popularity soared among the German people. In a single stroke, Stresa was revealed as a fiction, Locarno was jettisoned, and Versailles was dead. Germany had now taken a giant leap forward in her march toward revision and her preparations for war.

In March, reflecting on the public's delight, Viktor Klemperer noted in his diary:

> March 8, 1936: Hitler's new "act of liberation," the nation rejoices—what does internal freedom mean, what do we care about the Jews?

> March 23, 1936: It will be a tremendous triumph for the government. It will receive millions upon millions of votes. . . . Internal policies are forgotten. . . . . Martha Wiechmann, who visited us recently, pre-

viously completely democratic. Now [she says]: "Nothing has impressed me so much as rearmament and marching into the Rhineland." . . . Hitler said recently, "I am not a dictator. I have only simplified democracy."[55]

The Rhineland would almost certainly have been reoccupied by Germany with or without Neurath, and probably with or without Hitler for that matter. The question is whether it would have occurred in March 1936, or later, under more peaceful and stable circumstances.

Neurath's and Hassell's behavior during the Rhineland crisis demonstrates the premium placed on information and the value of its control. In the aftermath of the Night of the Long Knives, Neurath understood that failure to control information could prove costly. This recognition could only have been heightened by the ongoing political infighting and intrusions from Nazi Party interlopers, Ribbentrop primary among them.

We cannot know with certainty whether Neurath shared all the information at his disposal with the führer. We can, however, recognize that his motives for withholding data would have been substantial. In the frenzied atmosphere of Hitler's Reich, where neither one's career nor one's life was secure, intelligence stood at a high premium. Neurath's behavior in the months preceding the Rhineland crisis demonstrates that decision making in Hitler's Reich suffered not only from chaotic information flow but from a tendency toward risk fostered by the frenetic system that Hitler, himself, created.

Raising the Stakes
Information Flow and the End of Traditional Decision Making

4

Why did Neurath lose power so soon after his Rhineland coup? Constantin Freiherr von Neurath represented one of the last vestiges of traditional diplomacy in Hitler's Reich. While his leanings were undeniably nationalistic, he was not an avid Nazi, and other governments viewed him as a possible brake on Nazi extremism, at least in Germany's foreign policy. His removal from power marked the end of traditional decision making, a process under way since the Machtergreifung. Yet Neurath's fall was not preordained. As information control became an increasingly essential element in German foreign policy decision making, Neurath found himself outmatched by his rival Ribbentrop, who bested him in the battle for information.

One of Neurath's more daring maneuvers, both for the policy he advocated and the information he controlled, involved the Italo-Abyssinian war. Mussolini's invasion of Ethiopia in October 1935 was to have significant ramifications for Western Europe. The duce's actions forced an open split in the Locarno powers and estranged Italy from Britain and France, which in turn helped embolden Hitler to remilitarize the Rhine. But the Abyssinian crisis served another purpose for Hitler's Reich. The war distracted Western attention to Italy while Germany continued its covert rearmament program. Consequently, Germany had a strong incentive to see the war with Abyssinia continue.

The notion that Adolf Hitler, steeped in his avowedly racist dogma,

would ever have entertained the idea of supporting the Ethiopian military against Italy seems at first glance absurd. Nonetheless, it appears that Neurath encouraged the führer to back a covert plan to do just that. It also seems that some German weapons did make their way to Ethiopia in spite of official neutrality. The peculiar story of how these schemes unfolded highlights the value of information control, not only for matters of personal power but more vitally for questions of war and peace.

As early as 1934, the Ethiopian leadership found itself in a precarious position. Italy already wielded influence in the bordering regions of Eritrea and Italian Somaliland. The Ethiopian defeat of Italy at Adowa in 1896 left Italian nationalists thirsting for revenge. According to one historian, the duce wanted to conquer Ethiopia to show the Italian people that fascism stood for something grand and important.[1] Mussolini's rhetoric about recapturing the greatness of Rome's ancient empire convinced the Ethiopian government that it would have to modernize its forces to deter or defend against Italian aggression, and Germany appeared a likely ally and source of modern weapons. During Hitler's failed attempts to move on Austria in 1934, Mussolini had massed troops along the Brenner Pass, demonstrating his determination to defend Italian soil. Because Italo-German relations were tense, German-Ethiopian cooperation seemed a reasonable policy aim, both nations sharing a common foe.

In late October 1934, the Ethiopian emperor, Haile Selassie, made his first approach to the new German regime through the German envoy in Addis Ababa. On October 27, the envoy, Freiherr von Schoen, cabled Berlin that the Ethiopian emperor had requested permission to send a special representative to Germany to discuss the possibility of purchasing war materiel and airplanes. Apparently, the emperor understood the difficulties involved and requested a basic agreement between the two governments for cooperation.[2] Von Schoen advised giving a friendly response, but the emperor's initiative yielded no immediate results.

Two months later, on Christmas Day, the new German envoy, Unverfehrt, wired the Foreign Ministry with interesting news. Emperor Selassie had asked for a private audience with him and requested that no translators be present. According to Unverfehrt's report, the Ethiopian leader sought not only arms but chemical weapons as well. He urged that the two nations pursue closer relations and reiterated his desire to send a special representative to Berlin to conduct negotiations. Unverfehrt remained non-committal. He explained that the German government was not interested in becoming involved in the matter and politely suggested that Ethiopia would not benefit from German intervention.[3] Unverfehrt's report reached Berlin the following day, and Hans Dieckhoff immediately sent an unequivocal response. Unverfehrt was instructed to observe strict neutrality, to remain reserved in any further Ethiopian advances, and to make no offers of German mediation in Ethiopia's dispute. The Reich would not intervene.[4]

Neutrality was therefore the Foreign Ministry's official policy, and Neurath was responsible for its implementation. In spite of the official stance, Neurath either knowingly enabled some German weapons to find their way into Ethiopia, or he was unable to prevent their sale by a number of German firms. A Foreign Ministry official, Hans Frohwein, was charged to investigate the matter.

According to Frohwein's findings, reported in May 1935, the German Weapons Office (Waffenamt) had, in fact, permitted the delivery of some weapons to Ethiopia. However, these were said to be of little importance. The Waffenamt insisted that more vital weapons, such as artillery and machine guns, had definitely not been sent and could not be sent without its authorization. The Waffenamt admitted that it did not know exactly what military equipment had been delivered. It conceded that hand grenades might have been sold to Ethiopia by a small arms firm in Westphalia. In addition, Frohwein uncovered reports that German planes had been sold first to Egypt and then resold to Ethiopia. Although he concluded that these reports were unfounded, he acknowledged that it would be impossible to prevent aircraft from reaching Ethiopia through other countries. There were also allegations that German engineers and aircraft mechanics had traveled to Ethiopia, but Frohwein believed this untrue. Nonetheless, he added that the Air Ministry had asked the Interior Ministry not to issue travel visas for Ethiopia to such individuals.[5]

Frohwein's report demonstrates the limits on the Foreign Ministry's power to execute its policies. Whether the Waffenamt was forthcoming in what it knew and sincerely intended to assist the ministry in its policy of neutrality is uncertain. What is clear is that some individuals and firms had a considerable interest in circumventing official German foreign policy toward Ethiopia.[6] Whether Neurath knew of these violations and chose not to act, or whether he was limited in his ability to prevent them, is uncertain.

By the summer of 1935, the likelihood of an Italian attack on Ethiopia had increased substantially. Despite his previous failures to win German support, Emperor Selassie was not deterred. On July 17, the emperor's trusted representative, who was also chief of the Ethiopian army's armaments division, visited the former German representative in Addis Ababa, Kurt Prüfer, in the latter's Berlin flat. According to Bülow's account, the negus's representative had orders from the emperor himself to relate secret information on Ethiopia's military preparations and prospects in the event of war with Italy. The representative made clear that his nation's military was in dire need of modern arms. He also argued that Germany's and Ethiopia's interests were identical because Germany could not avoid a conflict with Italy over Austria. Both nations, therefore, had an interest in weakening Italy. The Ethiopian government was seeking a credit of three million Reichsmark for weapons procurement in Europe, an amount that would purchase roughly 30,000 guns and munitions and a sizeable number of machine guns.

There were, of course, a number of problems involved in granting Ethiopia a credit for arms procurement. Primary among these was that Hitler intended to woo Mussolini to his side. His long-term objective was to cultivate the Axis alliance, a partnership he had described as early as 1924, in *Mein Kampf*.[7] His immediate objective was to preclude Italian military intervention in the upcoming remilitarization of the Rhine. To this end, any support of Ethiopia would have had to be kept strictly secret. In contrast, Neurath viewed Italy as a rival for influence in Austria.[8] He did not envision an Italian alliance as compatible with Germany's southeastern European policy. Supporting the Ethiopians against Italy would therefore both weaken Italy's influence in Austria and divert Western attention from Germany's covert rearmament.

It is not clear who developed the plan to overcome this obstacle — the negus, his representative, Prüfer, or whether it was jointly concocted by all three. The proposed scheme operated along the following lines. Because the Ethiopians could not safely purchase arms within Germany without attracting attention and compromising German claims of neutrality, the Reich would transfer the funds to German industries such as Rheinmetall and Krupp, who operated branches in Switzerland and Sweden under different names (Solothurn and Bofors). Through these affiliated companies, the arms could be purchased and delivered. According to Bülow's report, Swedish and Swiss permission had already been obtained, but who had arranged this was not noted.

Bülow objected to the entire affair. Not only did he think that Germany should not provide arms to Ethiopia he also did not believe that secrecy could be maintained, recognizing that exposure would have damaging consequences for Germany's policies. Bülow viewed the need to rearm as essential to Germany's revisionist aims. If Germany's plan to sell arms to a foreign nation were discovered, it would not only damage relations with Italy and the other European powers but it could also jeopardize Germany's entire rearmament program. Nevertheless, he related Prüfer's report to the foreign minister.[9]

The traditional interpretation of Neurath during this episode portrays him as opposed to any intervention.[10] But this does not accord with a private letter Neurath wrote from his home in Leinfelden to Hitler just three days after Bülow's report. In this four-page letter marked "Top Secret," Neurath essentially reiterated Bülow's report to him, but, rather than expressing caution as Bülow had done, Neurath attempted to persuade the führer to fund the Ethiopian army.

> I cannot deny that the danger of an indiscretion cannot be completely excluded, even given great caution. On the other hand, the course of the Italo-Abyssinian war will be for European politics, and especially for the political issues of most importance to us, of such significance that I would like to propose that we comply with the Negus' request and provide him a three million Reichsmark credit for the purchase of weapons. If you share my view, I would contact the Finance Minister in order to arrange with him the provision of the three million Reichsmarks.[11]

Neurath explained to the führer how funds could be funneled to German arms manufacturers in Sweden and Switzerland to avoid complications. Although he admitted to some danger, Neurath argued that "the secrecy of the matter is secured because only the Negus and the agent, who happens to be the procurement head of the army, know of it. There would be no written or telegraphic correspondence over the matter."[12]

Hitler and President von Hindenburg, along with Papen, Neurath, and Schwerin von Krosigk, at Potsdam ceremonies.
Courtesy of Library of Congress. USZ-62-106471.

Vice Chancellor Franz von Papen among military personnel.
Courtesy of Library of Congress. USZ-62-130740.

Hitler and SA leader Ernst Röhm, rivals for the
military's allegience, oversee a soldiers' parade.
Courtesy of Library of Congress. USZ-62-42732.

Hitler reviews SA paramilitary troops. Note the soldiers'
unfit appearance and empty beer bottles in foreground.
Courtesy of Library of Congress. USZ-62-42728.

Nazi soldiers engulf an entire city street.
Courtesy of Library of Congress. USZ-62-42738.

Crowds flocking to cheer Hitler as he drives through
the Sudetenland following its seizure in late 1938.
Courtesy of Library of Congress. USZ-62-103049.

Ribbentrop and Stalin, along with Molotov, Schulenburg, and Hilger,
at signing of the Nazi-Soviet Non-Aggression Pact, 1939.
Courtesy of Library of Congress. USZ-62-101607.

Neurath not only intended to prevent foreign countries from discovering the scheme, he also appears to have kept Bülow in the dark as well. On August 3, 1935, more than two weeks after his initial note to the foreign minister, Bülow wrote to Neurath again to request an answer, reminding him "once more to bring the matter to the Führer's attention."[13] The negus's representative had once more sought the führer's approval and awaited a reply. The representative stressed that the end of the rainy season was soon approaching, the likely start of an Italian campaign. Therefore, any purchase of European weapons would need to occur immediately. Given Bülow's remarks, it appears that Neurath did not inform Bülow either of his support for the scheme or of his private letter to Hitler.

Neurath also requested that Hitler should not send an explanation of his views on the matter, but simply send a one-word reply. He concluded his letter to the chancellor: "It is sufficient to send me the word 'agreed' [einverstanden]. Because the agent will remain only a few more days in Berlin speed is advisable."[14] This would further attest to Hitler's reluctance to be linked to potentially unpopular or embarrassing affairs and his aversion to writing down directives on controversial issues. Neurath allowed Hitler the chance to support the scheme without committing himself in writing. It also permitted Neurath to avoid creating a documentary record of his own views. We cannot establish with certainty that Neurath actually sent this letter, but the detailed nature of his report and request to Hitler suggest that he did.

The traditional interpretation of Neurath's caution is based primarily on a document in which the foreign minister stated that Germany had remained neutral in the conflict.[15] However, Neurath made this assertion in a cable to Ambassador Hassell in Rome: "We have maintained complete reserve in the Abyssinian question and have, as you know, not only refuted the, mostly hysterical, Italian accusations, but have also met Italy's wishes in the matter of preventing any support of Abyssinia by the delivery of arms, etc."[16]

Since Neurath's letter to Hitler urging him to fund the Ethiopian resistance was written nearly one month after this comment to Hassell, it is possible that Neurath was sincere and that his thinking changed as the weeks passed. On the other hand, Neurath would have had a strong disincentive for revealing to Hassell any plans for German backing of Italy's enemy.

Not only did Hassell favor closer relations with Italy and surely would have opposed such a plan,[17] but Neurath's cable could have been intercepted by the Italian security service.[18]

As late as October 12, 1935, Neurath had still managed to persuade the chancellor against neutrality. In a memorandum to the Foreign and War Economy Departments of the Reich War Ministry, the Reich and Prussian Ministry of Economics, and the Reich Finance Ministry, West European Division Chief Gerhard Köpke wrote:

> With reference to the recent inter-departmental conference in the Foreign Ministry regarding a German ban on the export of arms, ammunition, and war materials to Italy and Abyssinia, I have the honor to state that the Führer and Chancellor, after hearing the views of the Foreign Minister, Freiherr von Neurath, has decided that for the present no declaration of neutrality of the kind discussed in the inter-departmental conference shall be made.[19]

According to the editors of the documentary collection, no record of this inter-departmental conference has ever been found.

By November 1935, Hitler had at last decided firmly on neutrality. In a minute by the director of the Foreign Ministry's Economics Department on November 7, the director noted Neurath's instructions to impose the ban: "Neurath told me of his conversation with Hitler on sanctions and the export of war material. I was instructed by Neurath and Bülow to tell Ernst [in the finance ministry] that 'the long proposed action on the Law on War Materials might now be taken.'" The director then noted that Ernst had said that the war and economics ministries had already agreed but the delay had resulted from foreign ministry objections.[20] No record of Neurath's discussion with Hitler on this matter has been found.

The November decision is corroborated by a memo dated July 2, 1936, in which an official in the Foreign Ministry's Trade Division noted that weapons sales to both Italy and Ethiopia had been forbidden since the previous November. Given the end of hostilities in East Africa, the official asked whether this restriction could now be lifted. Apparently, requests for finished infantry munitions were awaiting completion in the Waffenamt.[21]

Neutrality appears to have been the official German position after November. However, in January 1936, some individuals on both sides sought to circumvent the Waffenverbot. On January 28, the Ethiopian consul general wrote to Prüfer in the Foreign Ministry to ask if training planes and unfilled hand grenades could be delivered, since these items were not, in the strictest sense, war materials.[22] On February 8, Frohwein passed the Ethiopian request to the War Ministry, which responded on March 11. The official replied, "In the opinion of the Reich Minister for Air (Luftfahrt Reichsminister), training planes need not be considered war material."[23]

If the Ethiopians ever did succeed in acquiring German arms during the Italo-Abyssinian war, these weapons did little to aid their defense. General Debono's initial advance into Adowa proved relatively simple, but shortages of supplies and oil forced his armies to a halt by December 1935. His unwillingness to move more aggressively led Mussolini to replace him with General Badoglio. Meanwhile, the British and French foreign ministers attempted to appease the duce by offering the infamous Hoare-Laval agreement, which would have recognized Italian control over half of Ethiopia. Mussolini might have accepted the plan but Emperor Selassie would not. With the highly effective aid of mustard gas and germ warfare,[24] wholly unnecessary given Italy's overwhelming force, Italian troops marched on Addis Ababa. By the summer of 1936, Italian victory was complete and Emperor Selassie fled into exile.

What does this episode suggest about the foreign minister's role in foreign policy decision making? First, it appears that Neurath exerted influence over Hitler either to support the Ethiopian resistance or at least to forestall the imposition of a ban on the export of war material until November 1935. Second, it suggests a climate of distrust within the ministry. It seems that Neurath did not always inform Bülow and others in the ministry of his actual views on Germany's policy toward this conflict and that he related differing information to Hitler and to Bülow. Third, it is likely not coincidental that so few written records on the matter have been found. Neurath's behavior—his writing privately to Hitler from his home, his instructions to the führer to avoid setting his thoughts down in writing but instead to send only the word "agreed," combined with the curious absence of Neurath's own records of his discussions with Hitler over the affair— indicates a deliberate attempt to control information.

The more he could act as the conduit through which information flowed to Hitler and to his ministry colleagues, the more secure Neurath's position could remain. Put another way, being "the man in the know" enhanced his job security in a most uncertain climate. Precisely how uncertain his position had grown became increasingly apparent as the ministry underwent a significant transition.

In Neurath's battle to maintain control over information, a concurrence of factors combined to weaken his chances for success. One of those factors was embodied in his chief rival, Ribbentrop, who had set his sights on the post of state secretary, from where he hoped to direct policy and eventually supplant Neurath. In 1933, he had applied for the position, but Neurath found him severely lacking in ability and knowledge of history. Neurath's dislike of Ribbentrop soon became well known in ministry circles as the foreign minister did not dissemble his disgust at this "awful fellow" and his social pretensions.[25] Although the capable Bülow remained in his post, his health was poor.

Despite his disastrous trip to London in 1934, Ribbentrop remained undaunted. That year he was invited to a dinner hosted by the Foreign Ministry's protocol chief and, in accordance with protocol, was assigned a rather low seat at the table. Despite the fact that his rank did not warrant a higher place at the dinner table, Ribbentrop complained bitterly to Hitler that the men in the Foreign Ministry did not respect the Party. Hitler in turn complained to Neurath. Not wanting to slight the führer, Neurath ultimately agreed to grant Ribbentrop the title of minister in charge of disarmament issues and make his rank equal to that of ambassador. The agreement stipulated that Ribbentrop would be under Neurath's charge and would report directly to him.

In the two months following his appointment, Ribbentrop visited the foreign minister twice and the state secretary only once, even though his office was located across the street from the Wilhelmstraße.[26] Perhaps in Ribbentrop's view such visits were unnecessary, for it had now become possible for him to gain access to information by examining numerous cables between the Foreign Ministry and the German missions abroad. As a result, Bülow tried to deprive Ribbentrop of information, but with limited success. Erich Kordt, the conservative diplomat assigned to Ribbentrop's office, described the situation as follows:

> Because Ribbentrop in many cases rushed to Hitler with telegrams and obtained his decision before a thorough assessment could occur, Bülow often intentionally prevented Ribbentrop from gaining access to these telegrams. More often, however, Ribbentrop learned of their existence through the Reich Chancellery or through other means,

and he successfully complained to Hitler about his being inade-
quately informed by the Foreign Ministry. Bülow instructed me to do
my part to hinder Ribbentrop from interfering with affairs which
do not concern him.[27]

This resulted, Kordt explained, in a kind of continuous "mini-war," whereby
each successful sabotage of Ribbentrop's efforts to gain information led
him to complain to Hitler and thus gain the führer's sympathy.[28]

In March 1935, undoubtedly frustrated over his failure to control matters from outside the ministry, Ribbentrop again sought the position of
state secretary, but Neurath blocked him. Hitler responded by appointing
him on June 1 plenipotentiary of the Reich for special missions. This enabled him to represent Germany (much to Neurath's chagrin) at the naval
armaments limitation talks in London. Neurath and Ambassador Hoesch
fully expected that Ribbentrop's arrogant manner would produce the same
response from the British as it had in 1934. They assumed that the talks
would fail and that Ribbentrop's inability would at last be apparent to all.
Contrary to expectations, the British proved all too eager to sign an agreement limiting Germany's naval strength to thirty-five percent of Britain's.
Ribbentrop's triumphal return to Berlin won him praise from Hitler, respect from other Nazis, and consternation from the Wilhelmstraße.

Riding the tide of such a stunning success, Ribbentrop once again
pressed for the state secretary's post as Bülow's health continued to de-
cline. In the autumn, he proposed an alteration to the Foreign Ministry's
structure, which, if adopted, would have given him greater control over information than he or any other Foreign Ministry official had hitherto possessed. His aim was to chair a central operating committee to oversee competing Nazi foreign policy organizations such as the APA and AO. As state
secretary under this arrangement, Ribbentrop would chair the daily meetings while the foreign minister's role would be reduced to essentially a tit-
ular one.

Hitler's endorsement of this scheme triggered Neurath's immediate request to resign. In his resignation letter of October 25 he wrote:

I do not believe that Herr von Ribbentrop, even with the help of
trained officials, is able to fill (in a manner required by the country's
interest) this position, which demands an accurate knowledge of international relations, of the administrative machinery, and of the
available personnel. Since my person ought never, under any circum-

stances, to be a hindrance in the implementation of your views, I hereby resign the position first given to me by the late President von Hindenburg and renewed by yourself, and I request that you release me from my official duties as soon as possible.[29]

Neurath had demonstrated his value to Hitler, most notably during the Rhineland crisis, and the chancellor was reluctant to remove him. Ribbentrop was no substitute. The chancellor backed down on Ribbentrop's request, Bülow remained in his post, and Neurath, for the moment, retained control. But events were soon to overtake him. The führer appointed Ribbentrop to head the German delegation at a meeting of the Locarno powers in the aftermath of the Rhineland remilitarization. This enabled Ribbentrop to circumvent Neurath and report directly to the chancellor, while Neurath remained cut off from important information.

In one remarkable example of Neurath's desperate struggle for information, the foreign minister actually instructed Ambassador Hoesch to spy on Ribbentrop in order to learn of his rival's machinations. In a telegram of March 23, 1936, Neurath told Hoesch that he needed to know what Ribbentrop was communicating to Hitler from London as Ribbentrop was employing a special scrambling device for his cables.[30] While it is difficult to confirm whether Ribbentrop was in truth scrambling his messages to Berlin, it would not be surprising if he had, for he surely knew of Göring's Forschungsamt surveillance. As Erich Kordt's memoirs demonstrate, the office had at least once produced a verbatim text of one of Ribbentrop's telephone conversations. Only one month earlier, Neurath had employed a similar tactic by obtaining Ambassador Hassell's notes of his talks with Hitler before the ambassador cabled the official report to the ministry. It is indeed ironic that scarcely two weeks after his triumph in the Rhine, Neurath's need to gather and control information intensified rather than declined. The foreign minister understood that it was not sufficient to control the information at one's own disposal; to maintain one's position, it was also necessary to use whatever means available to discern the führer's will.

Neurath's steadily decreasing influence was exacerbated by the loss of five of his key Weimar-era colleagues. When the Nuremberg laws denied Jews the rights of citizenship on September 15, 1935, Meyer, a Jew who had ably headed the ministry's Political Division, and Köpke, the ministry's West European Division chief (who had a Jewish grandmother), were forced from office. No evidence suggests that Neurath held strong anti-Semitic views, for he worked alongside Meyer and other Jewish ministry officials for years. Yet when Meyer and Köpke were forced from office, neither Neurath nor Bülow, nor any other ministry colleagues, protested by resigning in solidarity. Neurath did, however, arrange for their pensions to be paid in foreign currency to help them emigrate should they wish.[31]

The ministry's loss of its Jewish officials was compounded by several unfortunate deaths. On April 10, 1936, Ambassador Leopold von Hoesch, who had served competently in London, unexpectedly died. Soon after, Ambassador Roland Köster in Paris also died. The most critical blow to Neurath's position came on June 21, when Bülow passed away. By June 1936, Neurath found his ministry suddenly depleted of five of its most capable diplomats, all men of Neurath's social ilk, trained in the traditions of German diplomacy. Not only did these changes reduce the quality of analysis within the ministry, they also left Neurath bereft of his key sources for inside information. Unable to rely on Hoesch or the others to inform him of Ribbentrop's activities, he lost potentially vital information. No longer could Bülow be called on to withhold information from Ribbentrop, and Bülow's post would have to be filled. Unfortunately for Neurath, Ribbentrop was keen to step in.

With Bülow's passing, Ernst von Weizsäcker remarked that the ministry had lost "the best horse in its stable." Weizsäcker, who had in 1936 succeeded Meyer as head of the Political Division, had the opportunity to observe matters closely from Berlin. In his memoirs, he noted the complete absence of any rational order to the flow of information:

> Normally the Government of a State receives its information in regard to foreign policy from the Foreign Ministry, which exists for that purpose. Apart from this it of course receives a mass of uncollated news from a variety of sources; this cannot be prevented, and there is no reason why it should be. But when it comes to taking decisions in foreign policy, the Government seeks the authoritative advice of the Foreign Ministry. And finally, the carrying out of the decisions reached is, and must be, in the hands of the Foreign Minister.
>
> In 1936 this normal state of affairs had in every respect already ceased to exist in Germany. Amateurish and irregular reports were often preferred to the official ones. Decisions were taken without the Foreign Minister or the Foreign Office having had a say in the fram-

ing of them. The carrying out of the decisions was entrusted to the most various quarters.[32]

A back-and-forth struggle for power now ensued. Believing he had come upon the master stroke that would finish Ribbentrop for good, Neurath persuaded Hitler to appoint Ribbentrop ambassador to Great Britain. Once Ribbentrop filled Hoesch's former post, Neurath reckoned that his rival would not only be far removed from decision-making in Berlin—and therefore cut off from information on policy matters—but would also fail in London where he was so disliked. This momentary setback to Ribbentrop's ambitions was quickly reversed. On July 24, the führer authorized Ribbentrop to continue his previous activities in addition to becoming ambassador, but added that Ribbentrop should report directly to him rather than Neurath. Once again, the foreign minister would be unable to keep track of his rival's activities. With no other cards to play, Neurath again tendered his resignation.

Hitler did not respond to Neurath's request to retire. On August 10 at the Olympic games, Neurath discussed the matter again with the chancellor. The result was a more normal arrangement whereby Ribbentrop was placed under Neurath's supervision. The victory was Neurath's, but it was to be a Pyrrhic one. In London, Ribbentrop did indeed fail to strengthen Anglo-German relations, but he succeeded in another diplomatic coup: the conclusion of the Anti-Comintern Pact, which paved the way for the future German-Japanese alliance.

To fill the vacancy created by Bülow's passing, Neurath appointed the career foreign service official Dieckhoff as transitional state secretary. Uncomfortable in this role, Dieckhoff requested transfer to Washington. Neurath consented and named him ambassador. During this period of transition, another crisis erupted that revealed the foreign minister's waning importance.

On July 17, 1936, a revolt broke out in Spanish Morocco and the following day spread to the Spanish mainland. General Francisco Franco, a leader of the rebels, requested German aid, in particular the provision of airplanes for the transport of troops. Franco's envoys reached Berlin on July 23 and met with Ernst Bohle of the AO. Lacking the authority to extend German aid, Bohle arranged a meeting with his superior, Hess, who in turn arranged for the envoys to meet with Hitler himself. On July 25, the führer received Franco's representatives in Bayreuth along with Göring, Blomberg, and one AO representative whom Hitler apparently ignored throughout the meeting. AO input was not a factor in Hitler's decision to assist Franco's rebels, nor were past contacts with Spanish fascists or the potential economic benefits of partnership. Hitler appears to have made his decision largely on an ideological basis, for he hoped to check the spread of communism.[33]

The decision to intervene in the Spanish civil war was taken without Foreign Ministry involvement. As Weizsäcker noted, "The news that Germany was to give aid to Franco's Spain took the Foreign Ministry by surprise."[34] On the same day that Hitler met Franco's representatives and decided to extend German aid, Dieckhoff outlined the ministry's opposition to involvement. Dieckhoff feared that German merchant ships operating in Spanish waters would be threatened if German arms sales to Franco's rebels were exposed.[35] As recently as the previous April, the German government had permitted the Krupp corporation to form two armaments deals with the Spanish Popular Front regime.[36] For Germany now to aid the Spanish rebels would, in Dieckhoff's view, have seemed inconsistent and unwise. Yet neither the Foreign Ministry's nor the AO's information mattered to Hitler.

Neurath's main contribution to the Spanish matter was limited to his counseling against a provocative military response to an unfortunate incident the following year. On May 29, 1937, unidentified planes bombed the German battleship *Deutschland*, which was serving as part of the Non-Intervention Committee patrolling the Spanish coast, resulting in the deaths of twenty-three sailors and the wounding of eighty-five others. Göring and Goebbels demanded massive bombing raids. Still able to exert some influence over his more hot-headed colleagues, Neurath persuaded them not to retaliate. It was agreed instead to increase German naval strength.[37]

Aside from this example of Neurath's modest input, Germany's involvement in the Spanish civil war, its sending of arms and military instructors, occurred largely without Foreign Ministry input. It represented Hitler's first major foreign policy decision that ran counter to Neurath's advice. As Hitler departed from more conservative revisionist aims and embarked on radical policies, Neurath's influence steadily eroded. However, the foreign minister's grip on power was slipping more because of his failure to maintain control of the information flow to Hitler.

Struggling to remain relevant, Neurath settled on Georg von Mack-ensen as Dieckhoff's replacement. Mackensen possessed two qualities that made him especially suitable. He had served in the ministry for many years but had joined the Nazi Party in 1933, which would placate the Nazis in the ministry's personnel department. And Mackensen was Neurath's son-in-law, sure to be trusted. Ironically, while Mackensen met Neurath's criteria for loyalty, Ribbentrop might have been the wiser choice. Had Neurath been able to overlook his personal animosity for his rival, he probably would have been in a much stronger position to control the information flow with Ribbentrop under his direct command. By bringing Ribbentrop into the ministry as state secretary, Neurath would have had a far greater chance of ascertaining what Ribbentrop was plotting, and he would have been in a better position to countermand Ribbentrop's directives or to force a confrontation and a choice over policy.

As control over information gained an ever higher premium, the inability to oversee and oppose Ribbentrop's activities significantly weakened Neurath's position. Sending Ribbentrop to London did not succeed, as Neurath had hoped, in removing his rival from the scene. Neurath had urged this appointment on the assumption that Ribbentrop would seek in vain to improve Anglo-German relations. In fact, Ribbentrop spent a full six-month period in 1936 without ever visiting his London embassy. Instead, he devoted much of his energies to ascertaining Hitler's will and being in the führer's presence. In contrast, Weizsäcker noted that "Neurath saw little of Hitler — much too little, in view of Hitler's tendency to act on the spur of the moment. With Hitler, anyone who was not on the spot did not count."[38] By allowing Ribbentrop to operate outside his control, Neurath consigned himself to ignorance, a situation that Ribbentrop exploited to outmaneuver his rival in determining foreign policy.

Upon appointing him ambassador to Great Britain, Hitler empowered Ribbentrop to form closer ties with Japan. By the close of 1936, Ribbentrop had brought Japan into the Anti-Comintern Pact. This step signaled a meaningful shift in Germany's Far Eastern policy, yet the foreign minister remained wholly ignorant of the move until Hitler had already accepted it. In protest, Neurath refused to be part of its signing. He struggled to explain to Hitler that the alliance with Japan would inevitably be interpreted as anti-British, and any hopes that the führer harbored of allying with England would be doomed to failure. Neurath's influence over the führer had by this point so significantly diminished that his counsel went unheeded.

On November 5, 1937, an event occurred that presaged a turning point in Germany's foreign policy. At a now infamous meeting, Hitler revealed his plans for a great war in the east. Gathering together the chiefs of the army, navy, and air force and the foreign minister, the chancellor laid out his plans for expansion and conquest of Lebensraum and called for the necessary military and economic preparations to ready the German nation for this historic mission. The adjutant who recorded this meeting, Colonel Hoßbach, failed to devote much attention to the ensuing debate, but what little record of it exists demonstrates Neurath's opposition.[39] The following day Ribbentrop brought Italy into the Anti-Comintern Pact, and a reconstitution of Germany's traditional alliance system was complete.

Neurath continued in his post for several more months, but his time was drawing nigh. In January 1938, the Blomberg-Fritsch affair erupted, in which the war minister and army chief of staff were implicated in allegations of sexual impropriety. The affair prepared the way for a series of personnel changes that would at last permit greater Party control over the army and diplomatic corps, the two state institutions Hitler had hitherto been unable to Nazify. On February 2, Neurath turned sixty-five and simultaneously celebrated his fortieth year of service in the ministry. Hitler attended the celebrations and the German press lauded Neurath as a devoted servant of the German nation. Two days later, Hitler summoned him to the chancellery to relieve him of his post.

Neurath's removal had by no means been a foregone conclusion. It occurred just as tension over the Austrian question was reaching its climax. The Anschluss, which occurred on March 12, 1938, proved to be one more major step in German foreign policy from which the Foreign Ministry was virtually excluded. Although the Blomberg-Fritsch affair provided an opportunity to supplant the remaining Weimar conservatives with Nazi Party faithfuls, the resilient Franz von Papen managed once again to escape a purge. On February 4, the same day that Hitler dismissed Neurath, the führer's state secretary in the Reich chancellery, Lammers, phoned Papen in Vienna to recall him. "I wanted to tell you this before you read about it in the newspapers," Lammers allegedly remarked.[40]

Fortunately for Papen, the lessons of June 30, 1934 had not escaped him. Realizing that his position rested in part on his ability to control the information flow to the führer and thereby make Hitler dependent on him, Papen traveled to Berchtesgaden the next day to speak with Hitler directly. There he explained to the führer that he had succeeded in getting the

Austrian chancellor, Kurt von Schuschnigg, to meet Hitler to discuss their differences, making it clear that his services were available to arrange a meeting if Hitler desired it.[41] Two days later Papen was back in Vienna, once more at work for the Third Reich, helping Hitler to achieve his next extraordinary coup, the bloodless annexation of Austria.

As for Neurath, his long struggle to retain authority in an ever more unstable environment had at last ended in defeat. His ever-loosening grip on the information arsenal contributed greatly to his loss of power. Neurath's removal in February 1938 did not represent an abrupt shift from traditional to radical foreign policy. Rather, his replacement by Ribbentrop only signaled the furthering of a process already under way for the previous five years. Traditional decision making did not end in Germany in 1938, but in 1933, with the advent of a Nazi regime and the tense domestic environment it produced.

Hitler's leadership style and the uncertain climate he engendered had led Neurath to take increasingly unorthodox measures in his conduct of foreign policy. Yet the appointment of Ribbentrop, a long-time Nazi Party faithful, did not reduce the level of risk taking. In fact, under Ribbentrop the degree of risks increased still further and with devastating consequences. From Ribbentrop to Weizsäcker (his new state secretary) down to the ambassadors, the Foreign Ministry became enmeshed in a tangled web of deception and disinformation, all in a desperate battle for information control — a battle that was to have dramatic implications for the outbreak of global war.

Betting
It
All
Disinformation, Deception, and the Anglo-German Talks

Following the German annexation of Austria, Hitler signed the Munich agreement in September 1938, along with Britain, France, and Italy. In March 1939, Hitler voided that agreement by invading Czechoslovakia. But while the attack on Prague demonstrated the regime's external aggression, between Munich and Prague a separate event within Germany exposed the Reich's internal violence. For several days beginning on November 7, 1938, the ever-mounting tension of life in a police state erupted into a maelstrom of destruction. German citizens burned down virtually every synagogue and ransacked and destroyed thousands of Jewish businesses and private apartments. By the close of Krystallnacht, ninety-one Jews lay dead, some 26,000 Jewish men were carted off to concentration camps, and thousands more were detained by authorities.[1]

There was nothing secret about Krystallnacht. It would have been impossible to conceal such extensive destruction across the country. Foreign journalists reported these events in newspapers around the world. No one in Germany, especially the well-informed diplomats in Berlin, could have avoided witnessing or at least learning about it. There could be no doubt in the diplomats' minds that they were living under a brutal regime, one capable of unleashing extraordinary violence against those it deemed undesirable.

After Krystallnacht, British public opinion of Germany only worsened, further diminishing the likelihood of an Anglo-German rapprochement. Hitler had hoped for an alliance with Britain as early as 1924, when he wrote that he saw Italy and Britain as Germany's natural allies.[2] Hitler believed that Germans and Britons, being of similar racial stock, had a historic mission. Britain had established a global empire; Germany should have an empire in Eastern Europe. The Anglo-German naval agreement of 1935 may have represented an initial step in this would-be alliance.

As late as 1938, Hitler appears to have maintained his hope of accord with Britain, or at least for British neutrality in Germany's expansion on the European continent, most immediately with regard to Czechoslovakia. That summer Hitler bypassed Ribbentrop and sent his personal adjutant, Wiedemann, to London for talks with the foreign secretary, Lord Halifax.[3] Whether Hitler at this point still harbored hopes of a British alliance is difficult to determine, but results were twofold. First, the move angered Ribbentrop and heightened his insecurity, for he found himself in the unpleasant position of having his ambassador in London, Herbert von Dirksen, aware of diplomatic maneuvers about which Ribbentrop was wholly ignorant.[4] Ribbentrop retaliated by bringing Wiedemann into the Foreign Ministry and transferring him first to the United States, and finally to Tientsin, China, thereby removing him from Berlin and precluding any chance of Hitler using that adjutant to circumvent him again. Second, it encouraged the belief, in both British and German circles in London, that Hitler actually still desired a British alliance.

Once Hitler invaded Prague, Chamberlain had little choice but to publicly abandon appeasement, despite his long-held conviction that it represented the best hope of bringing peace to Europe. After Prague, Chamberlain adopted a stronger stand in public toward German aggression, as typified by a speech he delivered in Birmingham on March 17. One of the prime minister's biographers noted, "Chamberlain's initial reaction was certainly one of profound disappointment, but the guarantees to Romania, Greece, and Poland arose not out of any conviction that his previous policy had been wrong, but rather out of the political and diplomatic situation created by Hitler's actions."[5] His public protestations notwithstanding, a number of private conversations continued between Chamberlain's closest adviser and German officials.

One of these conversations involved Arthur Bryant, a British historian, who had had prior contact with Dr. Kurt Blohm, an official in the British section of the foreign affairs department of Nazi headquarters. Blohm's direct superior was Walter Hewel, Hitler's staff officer. Chamberlain urged Bryant to meet with Blohm, but only under the strictest understanding that no one must know that he was acting at Chamberlain's behest, or even that Bryant had been in touch with the prime minister.[6] With Chamberlain's consent, Bryant succeeded in arranging two meetings in Salzburg with Hewel on July 11 and 12. The prime minister read Bryant's report on his conversations and minuted his comments to his close adviser, Sir Horace Wilson. Only after the matter had failed in Chamberlain's eyes to produce the basis for a general understanding did he instruct Sir Horace to inform Lord Halifax of what had occurred.[7]

The next series of secret talks took place from June to August. The principal players on the German side included Helmuth Wohlthat, Göring's chief economist in the Four-Year-Plan office, Theo Kordt, an official in the German Embassy in London, and Dirksen, the ambassador to Britain. In the personnel reshuffle during the Blomberg-Fritsch affair, not only was Neurath removed but ambassadors Hassell in Rome and Trautmann in Peking were recalled as well. Dirksen had initially been removed, but his mother, who had once worked to launch Hitler in Berlin society, arranged for her son's posting to London.[8] Thus, the diplomat who had served in Moscow during the end of Russo-German cooperation, and in Tokyo when Japan joined the Anti-Comintern Pact, now represented his country in London, at the point when Anglo-German relations reached their most critical stage of the inter-war period.

On the British side, the key actors included Prime Minister Neville Chamberlain; his adviser Sir Horace Wilson;[9] Foreign Secretary Halifax; Charles Rodan Buxton, a former parliamentarian; and Lord Kemsley, a newspaper proprietor.

Helmuth Wohlthat, an economist and Party member, headed Hermann Göring's office for the Four-Year Plan. Before 1939, Wohlthat had helped negotiate Nazi Germany's economic relations with Franco's Spain during the civil war and with Eastern European nations, especially Romania. Previously he had worked as an international entrepreneur, and through this experience had come to know London well. He had developed many contacts in Britain, including with Wilson. When in early June of 1939 he asked his chief for permission to pursue economic negotiations with Britain, Göring apparently gave him a free hand.[10] Göring's motivations might have stemmed from a desire to reach accord with England or from a wish to upstage Ribbentrop in foreign policy.[11]

Arriving in London, Wohlthat met with Sir Horace Wilson on June 6, not in Wilson's office, but at the private residence of the duke of Westminster. This venue allowed for greater secrecy, for Chamberlain could ill afford a public embarrassment over accusations that he was still pursuing appeasement.

The following day, a German who was not an official of the Reich government but who would become one of the leaders of the resistance movement, Adam von Trott zu Solz, met with Chamberlain in London. On his return to Berlin, Trott zu Solz submitted a report on his discussions, but Ribbentrop prevented it from reaching Hitler. The foreign minister also managed to block Trott zu Solz's reception by Göring.[12] Ribbentrop was intent on pursuing an alliance with Soviet Russia and had no intention of seeing those plans derailed, even if it meant denying Hitler access to information.[13]

Wohlthat and Wilson met again on June 7 and July 19 and 31, yet Wilson sent the foreign office a record of only one of these meetings. Wohlthat and Dirksen reported to Berlin that another Wohlthat-Wilson conversation occurred on July 21, but Sir Horace made no record of it and after the war denied that it ever took place. Wilson's record of the July 19 conversation depicted a nonchalant British willingness to consider serious German proposals for understanding, but Wilson noted that Wohlthat had not prepared any particular framework to discuss topics of mutual interest. "I did not press him to do this, as I was most anxious to maintain the position that had been adopted in the June conversation, namely that we were not unduly apprehensive about things and that the initiative must come from the German side."[14] Chamberlain initialed Wilson's report that same day without comment, demonstrating that the prime minister was aware of these German feelers.

One day later, July 20, Robert Hudson, British secretary of the Department for Overseas Trade, met Wohlthat and proposed wide-ranging offers for joint Anglo-German economic development of global markets, with particular regard to Russia, China, and Africa.[15] The *News Chronicle* caught wind of these new attempts by the government at economic appeasement of Germany and blasted the prime minister for his actions a few days later. On July 23, Chamberlain wrote privately to his sister of his anger at Hudson's indiscretion at permitting the press to learn of his talks with Wohlthat. He denied any knowledge or approval of Hudson's proposals. Whether Chamberlain, in conducting the correspondence with his sisters about political matters, was fully cognizant that he was creating a written record for future historians, or whether he simply trusted his sisters and wanted to share his thoughts and experiences on sensitive political matters with them, is uncertain.

According to both Wohlthat's and Dirksen's reports, Wohlthat met with Sir Horace again on July 21, when Sir Horace allegedly confirmed that Hudson's proposals represented official British government interest. Sir Horace then supposedly presented his interlocutor with a draft formula for Anglo-German cooperation, but this memorandum has never been found. Wohlthat's record of the July 21 meeting, as corroborated by Dirksen, alleged that Sir Horace made surprisingly generous offers. Dirksen wrote to Kordt that same day on the results of these discussions.

Sir Horace reportedly presented a detailed plan for Anglo-German accord that began with a proposal for a nonaggression pact. He said that Britain sought a renunciation of aggression as part of the agreement. Second, there would be a recognition of spheres of influence. Eastern and southeastern Europe were to be designated as Germany's sphere. Third, there would be agreements on arms limitations for land, sea, and air power. (Chamberlain had long sought an air pact with Germany, as this was a matter of particular concern for British security.)[16] Fourth, colonial issues would be resolved, including how best to develop Africa. The return of German property from her colonies was left unspecified, but would be addressed in later discussions. Further points included Germany's acquisition of raw materials, industrial markets, the exchange of financial facilities, and the regulation of international debts. Sir Horace Wilson said that the conclusion of a nonaggression pact would release Britain from her commitments to Poland; thus, the Danzig question would lose much of its importance for Britain.

Wohlthat enquired whether these proposals reflected official government policy, and Sir Horace replied that they had been discussed by important cabinet officials but that no firm decisions had yet been reached. At this point Sir Horace is said to have remarked: "The Führer need only take a blank piece of paper and list his demands and the British government would be prepared to discuss them." Wohlthat asked to whom he should give this paper in order to continue the discussions, and Sir Horace answered: "The decisive question in this relationship is that the Führer authorizes any person to speak on the above mentioned program. When the Führer has given such an authorization, the English government accepts any further form of negotiation." When asked whether Chamberlain had approved these plans, Wilson asserted that the prime minister had given his full consent.[17]

Sir Horace then discussed party politics with regard to the upcoming elections. He explained that it was irrelevant to the present government whether they used the slogan "Preparedness for War" or "Agreement with Germany." In either case, he asserted, the government would garner support and secure its existence for another five years. He stressed, however, that they preferred the peaceful path.[18]

At a cabinet inquiry in 1951, Sir Horace was asked if he had met with Wohlthat on July 21, to which he replied as follows:

> I have no recollection of such a meeting and doubt if it took place. . . .
> My book shows seven appointments on that day and there is no mention of Wohlthat. I had seen him three days earlier and had told him enough to make the position clear to him. I don't think he would have wanted to come again and it is extremely unlikely that, if he did, I gave him a "memorandum" such as is described.

Sir Horace further explained how contact with Wohlthat arose:

> I suggest that it is unnecessary to pay much attention to Wohlthat.
> He was not an accredited diplomatic representative and the only reason for explaining to him the British policy (determined rearmament but willingness to live at peace if Germany ceased to misbehave) was that Göring was his chief and that Göring was at that time thought to have a little influence with Hitler and to be perhaps a counterweight to Ribbentrop.[19]

Did Wohlthat simply invent Sir Horace Wilson's proposals in order to jumpstart an alliance,[20] or was he intensely ambitious, seeking to advance his career?[21] Or is it possible that Wilson intentionally failed to record

Wohlthat's visit in his journal precisely because of the matter's potentially embarrassing nature?

In the months prior to World War II's outbreak, various well-meaning interlopers meddled in Anglo-German relations hoping to prevent the looming crisis. Their ranks included an odd assortment, from millionaires to Australian air force pilots.[22] One of them differed in kind from the others: he was Charles Rodan Buxton, the former British parliamentarian with experience in foreign affairs.

On July 29, Theo Kordt reported that the retired Labor MP, Buxton, known for being pro-German and in favor of conciliation, visited him to discuss Anglo-German understanding. According to Kordt, Buxton stressed the need to return to secret diplomacy, given the agitated state of public opinion. Buxton then laid out a carefully enumerated plan for dividing the world into spheres of influence and began by making curious analogies to the Anglo-French treaty of 1904 and the Anglo-Russian treaty of 1907. In the case of the former, Buxton explained, France had challenged Britain's control over Africa, but the dispute was settled by agreeing on separate spheres of influence. In the latter treaty, Russia had challenged Britain in Persia, Afghanistan, and Tibet, and again a division of spheres of influence had maintained the peace. Buxton proposed that the time had come for another such arrangement.[23]

Buxton's proposals closely resembled Wilson's of July 21. Both spoke of spheres of influence and noninterference. Both designated east and southeast Europe as the German sphere. Both accepted Britain's release from any obligations to states within the German sphere. Both urged German cooperation in Europe and entrance into arms limitation agreements. The proposals differed in that Buxton mentioned that Britain would work toward having France renounce her pact with Czechoslovakia and her ties with Eastern European states. Buxton also expressly stated that Britain would abandon its proposed alliance with Moscow and requested that Bohemia and Moravia eventually be granted a degree of independence.[24] If Buxton was acting independently, he managed to concoct an astonishingly similar plan to the one Sir Horace Wilson allegedly advanced on July 21.

The other possibility is that Kordt fabricated Buxton's proposals in order to make them resemble those related by Wohlthat and Dirksen. Theo Kordt and his brother Erich, both senior diplomats, were strong opponents of the Nazi regime. That Theo Kordt might have risked much to join

Wohlthat's and Dirksen's conspiracy is conceivable. There is, however, one peculiar coincidence to be explained.

On August 1, Ambassador Dirksen noted in a report to Weizsäcker that Chamberlain, in a speech before the House of Commons, had referred to the Anglo-French treaty of 1904 and the Anglo-Russian treaty of 1907, though in a different context from that in which Buxton had done. It struck Dirksen as peculiar that two men, Buxton and Chamberlain, wholly independent of one another and within a forty-eight-hour period, would conjure up references to both of these treaties. Even if Kordt had been part of the conspiracy to fabricate British overtures, how could he have known on July 29 what Chamberlain would say before the House of Commons two days later?[25] This had to be a remarkable coincidence, as it enabled Dirksen to suggest to his superior that Buxton's proposals were originating from higher up. According to Kordt's report, he pointedly asked Buxton if he, Buxton, had discussed his proposals with cabinet officials, but Buxton refused to answer directly.[26]

Given that both Buxton and Chamberlain referred to the treaties, it is plausible that Buxton had been instructed by the prime minister. It is also possible that Chamberlain intentionally made this public reference as a signal to the Germans, hoping Dirksen would do precisely what he did, namely, report to Berlin that Buxton's proposals appeared to be emanating from Downing Street.

Still another unofficial contact occurred outside the British Foreign Office. Lord Kemsley, the British owner of Allied Newspapers and a strong supporter of Chamberlain's policies, had been invited to Berlin by the German press chief, Otto Dietrich. On July 20, Sir Horace briefed Kemsley on what to say in the event that he should meet with important German officials. On July 27, Hitler himself received Kemsley for a one-hour conversation in the Wagner House at Bayreuth. According to Kemsley, Hitler had claimed no interest in Robert Hudson's proposals because it was not money (a reference to Hudson's offer of a substantial loan) that Germany sought. Hitler did suggest that each country should put its demands on paper and that this might lead to a discussion.[27]

If Hitler was truly interested in negotiations, and if he had mentioned the Hudson-Wohlthat talks, why did he not also refer to Wohlthat's meeting with Wilson on July 21? Dirksen and Wohlthat had both sent reports to Göring and Ribbentrop, respectively, detailing Sir Horace's invitation for the führer to list his demands and authorize a negotiator. Even if Dirksen and Wohlthat had jointly invented these offers, they did send their reports to Berlin.

There are several feasible explanations for Hitler's curious silence on this point. One is that he viewed Kemsley as too unofficial a contact with whom to discuss Wilson's secret proposals. If this had been the case, however, why would Hitler have suggested that *both* parties write down their demands after Wilson had already given Hitler a free hand to set the terms for discussions? It would have been wholly uncharacteristic for Hitler to have given the upper hand to his opponents. Another explanation is that Hitler intentionally wanted to confuse Chamberlain and maintain the fiction of a possible peaceful settlement, but this would also not explain his failure to mention Wilson's proposals. A third explanation is that Hitler simply was not interested, but it is clear from Hitler's actions since 1938 that he wished to avoid British intervention in his war on Poland. Even in the final hours before the outbreak of hostilities, Hitler still sought British neutrality. A fourth possibility is that Hitler never knew of the alleged British offers. Wohlthat only made his report on July 24, and it is possible that Göring either had not read it by the time of Hitler's meeting with Kemsley or had yet to discuss it with the führer.

Ribbentrop, for his part, failed to read Dirksen's reports on the matter. Once he learned of the talks, the foreign minister scrambled to gather information about them. On July 31, Ribbentrop wired Dirksen in London requesting immediate reports on the Hudson-Wohlthat talks.[28] Weizsäcker then also wired Dirksen informing him that Wohlthat's report had gone first to Göring and later to Ribbentrop. It is possible that Göring intentionally delayed sending Ribbentrop the Wohlthat report as part of their ongoing struggle for influence over foreign affairs. It is also possible that Göring withheld this information because he himself was uncertain about political agreement with Britain and wished to control the information on the matter. Whatever the reason for the delay, Weizsäcker confirmed that Wohlthat's report included Sir Horace's wide-ranging proposals for political, military, and economic cooperation. The state secretary remarked that it appeared that England was extending a serious feeler.[29]

Dirksen replied to Ribbentrop that same day. He explained that he had already reported on Wohlthat's conversations with Hudson and Wilson and cited his previous telegrams. Leaving no room for misinterpretation, Dirksen wrote, "We can firmly say that the tendencies observed to date have intensified beyond mere economic plans and are either being worked on directly by Chamberlain or at least are approved by him." Dirksen then reiterated what he had earlier reported to Berlin:

a. War is certain if we do not address these issues.
b. The English encirclement endangers the peace.
c. English rearmament to seek parity with Germany is an attempt to conceal Britain's weakness.[30]

But Dirksen could not convince Ribbentrop that Britain would honor her commitments to Poland and not remain neutral in event of war. Ironically, even if Dirksen, Wohlthat, Weizsäcker, and Kordt had all collaborated to fabricate British proposals and lure Hitler into negotiations, Hitler appears never to have learned of what was being offered.

On July 31, Chamberlain met with Kemsley to discuss the latter's encounter with Hitler. That evening Chamberlain gathered Wilson, Lord Halifax, and Sir Alexander Cadogan, permanent under-secretary of state for foreign affairs,[31] to review the situation. Chamberlain then instructed Kemsley to pass a message to Hitler via Dietrich asking the führer to list his demands.[32]

Three days later, Sir Horace met privately with Dirksen. In Sir Horace's account of this meeting, he claimed that the German Embassy requested that the meeting be held in Sir Horace's apartment. According to Sir Horace, he told Dirksen nothing that had not already been explained to the Germans publicly: that Germany must take positive steps toward rebuilding the good will destroyed in March, such as relieving the pressure on Danzig or declaring eventual autonomy or home rule for Bohemia and Moravia.[33]

Dirksen's account of his August 3 meeting with Wilson paints a very different picture. The ambassador reported that Wilson confirmed all the offers he had previously made to Wohlthat and now elaborated on each point in greater detail. The nonaggression pact would be a bilateral agreement between Britain and Germany. The accord would release Britain from her commitments to Poland and negate her alliance plans with Soviet Russia. Wilson stressed that the utmost secrecy had to be maintained lest the cabinet be forced to resign. When Dirksen expressed skepticism over the likelihood of any British cabinet gaining support for such a pact with Germany, Wilson insisted that the British public could be persuaded if the führer would show signs of relaxing the situation by seizing the peace initiative.[34] When Dirksen asked how talks could continue given the British government's need for total secrecy, Sir Horace replied that meetings could be held inconspicuously in Switzerland. Wilson emphasized that this was an official feeler by the British government to which a German response was awaited.[35]

With war approaching, time was of the essence, and Foreign Secretary Halifax was next to come forward with a plea. On August 9, Dirksen visited Halifax before the ambassador planned to depart for Berlin. According to Dirksen's own account, he complained to Halifax that the democratic states were not prepared to resolve outstanding differences because of their uncontrolled presses, and he cited the Hudson incident that had jeopardized the Wohlthat mission. Halifax replied that he had thought the Munich Accord had established a fifty-year peace in which Germany would be the predominant power on the continent, but Hitler's aggression since then had shaken the British public's trust. Halifax contended that Chamberlain could gain support in the House of Commons either for a war with Germany or for an agreement. At present, most British citizens were distrustful of Germany, he asserted, but they strongly desired peace. A period of calm could allow for a change in public opinion after which it would be possible to discuss peace.[36] Halifax may have been hoping that a few weeks of calm would force a postponement of any further German aggression until after the coming September rains and ensuing winter, thus gaining a full six-month reprieve for Britain. That period of calm was not to come.

Despite all the efforts to interest Hitler in negotiations, it appears that the chancellor never received a full or accurate account of what was being offered.[37] Although Göring met three times with Hitler during this period, it is impossible to know whether he accurately reported on Wilson's alleged offers, if he raised them with the chancellor at all. If Göring failed or was unwilling to deliver Wilson's proposals to the führer, Dirksen, who had no direct line to the chancellor and had to work through Ribbentrop, had little chance of success. Recalled to Berlin, the ambassador made one final attempt to inform Hitler of Chamberlain's secret intent.

One week after his talks in Wilson's apartment, Dirksen arrived in Berlin and attempted to see Ribbentrop:

> I requested of the gentlemen in the Ministry to report my arrival in Berlin to the Foreign Minister and to ask when and if I should come to Fuschl to report. Over the next few days I was told that no reply had come from the Foreign Minister. Nevertheless I asked State Secretary Weizsäcker when I could report to the Foreign Minister in Fuschl. Herr von Weizsäcker said it was possible for him to inform the Foreign Minister by post that I requested an interview. He [Weizsäcker] later read me a section from his letter to the Foreign Minister wherein my report was summarized, in particular the position of England in event of a German-Polish war.
>
> During these days I was repeatedly told that the Foreign Minister was convinced that England would not participate on Poland's side in the event of a German-Polish war. I further learned that Wohlthat's report over his London talks were viewed more as general impressions. My report over my talks with Sir Horace Wilson were seen as a further sign of England's weakness.
>
> A reply from the Foreign Minister did not come. It was clear that he had neither the time nor the wish to hear my report.[38]

During the days spent waiting for an audience with the foreign minister, Dirksen dropped by Wohlthat's office for a visit, but Wohlthat had gone on vacation. Later that month on August 25, Wohlthat wrote to Dirksen to apologize for having been on vacation when Dirksen had stopped by. Wohlthat noted that his report over the Wilson proposals had gone from Göring to Ribbentrop but that it had been interpreted more as a sign of the general atmosphere in Britain.[39] On August 27, Dirksen replied that he had been able to confirm the contents of Wohlthat's conversations with Sir Horace Wilson and to obtain further information, but remarked that he could only await further instructions from Berlin.[40]

Why did Wohlthat, on one of his rare opportunities to meet with Dirksen, choose to go on vacation, especially at a moment when their scheme to lure Hitler into negotiations with Britain had reached a critical juncture? Dirksen's and Wohlthat's failure to coordinate a meeting at such a pivotal time underscores how little contact they actually had. Herbert von Dirksen was a career diplomat who spent the 1930s on three major postings, as ambassador to Moscow, Tokyo, and finally London. Helmut Wohlthat worked in a Berlin office building on economic questions as Göring's chief of the Four-Year Plan. Given the sheer physical distance between them, these two men had little chance to meet, come to know and trust each other, and hatch what can only be viewed as an imprudent plan. In the uncertain atmosphere of Hitler's Reich, where men were scrutinized, arrested, or murdered for far lesser offenses than treason, trust in one's collaborator would have been essential. Since there is no record of long or sustained contact between these two men, and much to suggest that their opportunities for contact were limited, it is surprising that they would have taken such risks without a strong foundation of trust between them.

If Dirksen and Wohlthat were conspiring to fabricate British proposals, then they were taking enormous personal risks for questionable gains. If Hitler had accepted the British offers to negotiate, the moment Hitler's special envoy arrived in London—or Switzerland—Chamberlain and Wilson would have insisted that they had never made any offers to negotiate. Dirksen and Wohlthat would have been immediately exposed. Either the conspirators were gambling their careers, and possibly their lives, on a plan that could scarcely succeed, or the Chamberlain-Wilson proposals were for real.

Shortly after the outbreak of war, Dirksen retired to his estate at Gröditzburg, where he compiled a thirty-page review of Anglo-German relations throughout his tenure as ambassador in London. In this summary he recapitulated events concerning Chamberlain's, Wilson's, and Hudson's proposals and his unsuccessful attempts to discuss them in person with Ribbentrop. This survey matches the information contained in his, Wohlthat's, and Kordt's records of July and August. Having completed this thorough review, Dirksen closed it in his personal files and sent it to no one. If Dirksen had been falsifying Sir Horace's offers, he went to considerable trouble to make an additional record of his conspiracy:

> I have prepared the above review because I felt obligated to preserve in writing the development of the German-English relationship as it occurred during my tenure of duty in the event that later the desire should be awakened to collect all available material on this matter. This responsibility weighed all the more heavily on me as all impor-

tant documents of the London Embassy had to be burnt shortly prior
to the war's outbreak and the reports to the Foreign Ministry did not
contain some particulars.[41]

98   After the war, Dirksen elected to forego a chance to reveal his conspiracy at a time when so many others who had served the Nazi regime were
anxious to present themselves as having engaged in acts of resistance. In
his memoirs written in 1949, Dirksen recounted the Anglo-German secret
negotiations precisely as he had recorded them a decade earlier. He could
have chosen to reveal his cabal against the führer and describe how he tried
to thwart Hitler's war by luring him into talks with the British. Instead,
Dirksen maintained his position as having accurately related genuine
Chamberlain-Wilson pact proposals.[42]

Unable to gain an audience with Ribbentrop, Dirksen decided to send
yet another report summarizing his previous cables and stressing his conviction that Britain would fight to defend Poland. On August 18, he sent
his report to Weizsäcker, who, at Dirksen's behest, forwarded it to the foreign minister. Dirksen then asked Weizsäcker's permission to remain available at Gröditzburg, but as the ambassador noted, "My services were no
longer required."[43]

Ribbentrop had strong reasons for not wanting to meet with Dirksen.
Dirksen had expressed to the Italian ambassador in Berlin, Bernardo Attolico, his frustration over Ribbentrop's machinations, but having resided
outside of Germany for so long, he was not sufficiently alert to the dangers
of freely expressing one's opinions over the telephone or by cable. Attolico
wired the ambassador's remarks back to Rome, but Nazi officials intercepted and deciphered his cable and showed it to the foreign minister.[44]
Ribbentrop, enmeshed in political rivalry, had no tolerance for an aristocratic career diplomat who questioned his ability.

Beyond his personal distrust of Dirksen, Ribbentrop stood on the
brink of his greatest triumph, and Dirksen's news threatened his success.
Ribbentrop's own agenda involved an alliance with the Soviets and a war
against the Western powers.[45] The Nazi-Soviet pact represented the crown-
ing moment of his career. It was the coup he had long hoped to secure, and
it brought him the accolades of Hitler he coveted. The last thing he would
have wanted to hear was news of Britain's willingness to sign a nonaggression pact with Germany. For this reason, Ribbentrop had to insist

that Britain would not fight over Poland, lest Hitler doubt the wisdom of a pact with Stalin. On August 11, Italian Foreign Minister Ciano met Ribbentrop at Schloss Fuschl, where the latter insisted the West would not fight over Poland. Ciano left this ten-hour meeting convinced that Ribbentrop intended to provoke a war. The following day, Ciano saw Hitler, who parroted Ribbentrop's conviction.

Because it was in Ribbentrop's interest to portray the British proposals as representing a general atmosphere of weakness, he likely never showed Hitler Dirksen's report of the August 3 meeting with Sir Horace. If he had, Hitler would probably have referred to Wilson's offers to negotiate once Britain's intent to defend Poland became apparent. Hitler never mentioned it. Ribbentrop had effectively blocked Dirksen's information from reaching the chancellor.

Just two weeks before the outbreak of war, the Anglo-German talks reached their finale. Whether he had proposed them or not, Chamberlain finally received a response to his or Sir Horace's secret overtures. On August 20, Fritz Hesse, the German Embassy adviser, wrote to Sir Horace on Ribbentrop's instructions. The German government, Wilson was told, had no interest whatsoever in negotiations with Britain.[46] There is no evidence that Hitler instructed Ribbentrop to send this belated reply.

On August 22, the British cabinet assembled to discuss Britain's response to the growing numbers of German troops along Poland's borders. Chamberlain's personal letter to Hitler, worked on by many hands, had to show firmness. With the conclusion of the Nazi-Soviet pact, even a hint of appeasement at this point could prove catastrophic.

Although Hitler's timetable called for operations against Poland to commence on August 25, he delayed the attack once he learned that the British had signed their mutual assistance treaty with Poland and that Mussolini would remain a bystander. Ribbentrop's confident assertions were proving wrong. But Hitler continued his efforts to keep Britain out of the war. His demands to British ambassador Nevile Henderson, wholly insincere and impossible to meet, were entertained briefly in London but rejected in Warsaw. Poland resolved to fight. France resolved to stall. Chamberlain lacked resolve altogether.

On August 27, Oliver Harvey, Halifax's personal secretary, noted in his diary, "I am terrified at another attempt at a Munich and selling out of the Poles," but he feared that Wilson and R. A. Butler were "working like beavers for this."[47] On August 28, Cadogan recorded in his diary that Nevile Henderson, apparently in consultation with Chamberlain and Halifax, intended to offer a nonaggression pact to Germany, but Cadogan succeeded in discouraging such an offer at this stage:

> Last night H[alifax] and N[evile] H[enderson] rigged up some instructions to NH for guidance in his talk with Hitler. At NH's suggestion, they included offer of Non-Aggression Pact with Germany! I managed to kill this with P[rime] M[inister] and H.[48]

Poland was unable and unwilling to meet Hitler's sixteen demands. The führer thus informed the German public that Polish refusal to negotiate compelled him to launch the war. Even after the war's outbreak, when Britain's commitments to Poland should have commenced immediately, Ciano presented Hitler with another chance to gain ground in Poland while forestalling Allied intervention. While the Polish foreign minister, Colonel Beck, pleaded with Britain for air strikes on Germany's western front to draw off some German fire, Ciano proposed a five-power conference to discuss the Polish question. Georges Bonnet, the French foreign minister, encouraged this alternative, British leaders debated, and Hitler promised to respond by September 3.

On September 2, the cabinet demanded that Germany meet a time limit for withdrawal from Poland or Britain would declare war. Contrary to his ministers' wishes, Chamberlain informed the House of Commons that evening that no time limit had yet been set and no agreement had been reached with France. Arthur Greenwood, the deputy Labor leader, spoke, reflecting the general disgust with these delays in declaring war. Chamberlain, still desperate to avoid a full-scale conflagration, had no more cards to play.

Later that evening either Hitler or Ribbentrop made one more attempt. In a secret meeting with Sir Horace, Fritz Hesse recorded that he proposed a German withdrawal and payment of reparations to Danzig if Britain would agree to mediate. Wilson's version differs somewhat. He recorded that the Germans suggested that he travel to Berlin in secret to discuss the entire matter with Hitler personally. Sir Horace maintained that he stood firm. Regardless of what was actually proposed, no British leader could at that time have dared any final appeasement, especially as Chamberlain was facing a cabinet revolt. A core of Chamberlain's ministers, including

Sir John Simon and Leslie Hore-Belisha, staged a sit-down strike in a room in the House of Commons. When called to confront the prime minister, they expressed their disappointment that Chamberlain's public announcement had not included the time limit on German withdrawal that they had called for in the previous cabinet meeting. The pressure on Chamberlain precluded any action other than war.

Even after Henderson delivered the British declaration on September 3, Hitler made one final attempt to avoid British entry. The Swedish intermediary, Birger Dahlerus, phoned Halifax to ask if Göring could fly to London to discuss the situation.[49] Frank Roberts, a prominent diplomat in the Foreign Office, received the call but, believing it unworthy of relating, decided not to inform Halifax at all. The time for talk had ended. War had begun.

Someone sought to lure Hitler into talks on the eve of war. Whether it was Chamberlain and Wilson, or Dirksen and Wohlthat, their plan failed because it assumed that Hitler would receive the information they were sending. They did not understand that Hitler's regime fostered internal deception and manipulation of information. They did not comprehend that information control not only equaled power, it also affected the decision for war.

**Hitler's
Trump
Card**
Information Gaps
and the
Nazi-Soviet
Pact 6

Although the secret Anglo-German talks never produced any concrete agreement with Britain, they may have contributed inadvertently to the conclusion of a wholly different alliance. While the Wilson-Wohlthat talks were occurring in London, two other sets of negotiations were taking place. One was between Britain, France, and the Soviet Union for a triple alliance aimed at military cooperation to counter German aggression. The other was between German and Soviet representatives over the fourth partition of Poland. The Nazi-Soviet pact was Hitler's last diplomatic move before the war, and it represented his most infamous foreign policy coup.

On August 23, 1939, Nazi Germany and Soviet Russia signed a nonaggression pact, which secretly determined each nation's spheres of influence in Eastern Europe and paved the way for the outbreak of World War II. The Nazi-Soviet pact remains one of the most significant diplomatic events in the twentieth century, for its conclusion both fostered World War II's outbreak and contributed to distrust of Soviet intentions during the Cold War. While the pact's genesis has been hotly debated for more than sixty years, many unanswered questions still remain. Why did Stalin sign a pact with Hitler when he knew that Hitler intended to attack Russia? Wouldn't Stalin's interests have been better served by allying with Britain and France to offset Hitler's power? But the riddles are not limited to Stalin's behavior. They also include the manner in which information flowed within Germany and what Hitler knew of Stalin's overtures. And they necessarily pertain to Chamberlain as well. Why did the British prime minister, knowing that secret Nazi-Soviet discussions were under way, not make any serious efforts to reach accord with Stalin? What were Chamberlain's intentions regarding the Soviets and the Germans and how did *his* actions contribute to the pact's formation?

The pact's origins are intimately linked to information gaps, leaks, and silence from several capitals, and Soviet intelligence may have played a crucial role. Russians spy extremely well. For much of the twentieth century the Soviet secret service frequently penetrated its adversaries' defenses with skill and tenacity, and the prewar period was no exception. Already by September 1934, agents from the NKVD had penetrated Hitler's security, ascertaining the details of a meeting between Count Friedrich Werner von der Schulenburg (the German ambassador to Moscow) and the chancellor. On September 4,[1] a special agent reported on Schulenburg's meeting in Nuremberg with Hitler and Alfred Rosenberg, head of the Außenpolitisches Amt, to discuss the instructions Schulenburg received from the Foreign Ministry to encourage "correct" relations between Germany and Russia by any means.

By 1935, the NKVD appears to have bugged the embassy with listening devices. On May 11 notes detailed a meeting in the German Embassy between Schulenburg and newly arrived Party officials from Germany. During the course of the conversation, one of the Nazi officials announced that in the near future a completely new radio device of special construction would arrive from Germany to be used for establishing the exact location of secret Soviet radio stations. Schulenburg's subordinate, Fritz Tvardovsky, already familiar with these devices, expressed his delight and called them "remarkable machines" with whose aid "Germany has already managed to discover many secrets." Ironically, as the Nazi officials were lauding the sophistication of their new espionage equipment, the Soviets appear to have been listening to their every word.

NKVD surveillance of Schulenburg was so thorough that they not only made detailed records of his conversations and whereabouts, as well as his tendency to drink heavily, but on one occasion also believed they had uncovered a Gestapo plot against him. In an internal report in 1936 to NKVD Director Yezhov, agent Volovich described an incident in which the

German ambassador's brakes failed just as his car was traveling along a mountain pass. According to Volovich, Schulenburg's bodyguards leapt from the car and held it back from sliding over the precipice. Volovich suggested that Yezhov have the Special Division of Intelligence investigate this incident further because of information they possessed that the Gestapo had planned an "accident for the ambassador." Volovich wrote that Schulenburg's driver at the time his brakes failed was a known Gestapo agent. If the Gestapo was indeed plotting to eliminate Schulenburg, or even if Soviet intelligence only believed this to be the case, then the NKVD found itself in the curious position of having to protect the German ambassador from his own government. Such protection was necessary if the Soviet Union wanted to avoid being caught in an uncomfortable incident that would further strain relations, especially at a time when the USSR was engaged in purges.

On another occasion, German diplomats arrived at their offices one morning to discover a broken key jammed in the lock of the safe containing their most sensitive materials. They could not establish whether the key had been broken upon opening or closing of the safe. After the war, Gustav Hilger (a long-time German adviser in the Moscow embassy) learned from an NKVD agent that the operation to obtain secret documents had failed that night, but that they had often obtained them from the night watchman, who was an insider.[2]

The NKVD obtained much of the information that flowed between Moscow and Berlin. Cables were frequently intercepted, meeting rooms were bugged, and informants worked within the building. One such informant even gained access to sensitive material relevant to Operation Barbarossa just prior to the German attack — information that Schulenburg had left on his desk after an evening of heavy drinking. Soviet intelligence reports can now help shed light on how and when the Nazi-Soviet rapprochement developed.

Although there has been no consensus on the exact date when Germany and Soviet Russia first considered accord, both Hitler and Stalin appear to have contemplated rapprochement prior to the generally accepted dates in 1938 and 1939. There is strong evidence that both leaders were keeping options open throughout the 1930s. Although Hitler did not immediately terminate relations with the Soviets upon coming to power, the first year of his rule saw diminishing trade with the USSR and the end of military cooperation with the Red Army. Nevertheless, the Comintern did not adopt an anti-fascist line until 1935, and confidential political discussions under the pretext of trade talks occurred sporadically from 1935 to 1937, led by David Kandelaki, the Soviet trade representative in Berlin. While Göring and Hjalmar Schacht participated in these discussions, they never resulted in détente. Kandelaki likely was acting on Stalin's personal instructions, as Yevgeny Gnedin, then Soviet press secretary in Berlin, noted in his postwar recollections.[3]

Schulenburg appears to have been working for rapprochement even prior to the Munich agreement of 1938. Numerous signals were emanating from the ambassador and from Hitler himself that a shift in relations could be in the offing. In a report dated April 14, 1937, NKVD agents learned of a meeting in Schulenburg's house, during which the ambassador discussed his talks with Hitler of the previous month. According to these records, Hitler and Schulenburg first addressed the German leadership's decision over the future introduction into Spain of only instructors and military technology. The report then related Hitler's concern over Germany's economic situation in connection with serious difficulties regarding raw materials. Hitler directed Schulenburg to continue the previous policy of preventing a split in relations with the Soviets, while not allowing steps toward closeness.[4]

In a meeting between Schulenburg and an unidentified individual who was working for the NKVD, the agent noted Schulenburg's planned trip to Berlin for discussions with Hitler and related the ambassador's comments:

> There is a subtle shift in the field towards finding some sort of firm basis for improving these [Russo-German] relations. Of course, this is not much, but given our relations, it is a positive step. If among the leadership there is great hostility towards Russia, then among the Reichswehr and some influential financial and _____ [word indecipherable] circles are very concrete tendencies towards the improvement and stabilization of relations. If this shift becomes reality, then it is necessary to consider economic negotiations as the beginning of this positive period, after which would follow political negotiations. As far as I could understand from conversations with Litvinov, who is, as is known, a great supporter of Germany, today he is also envisioning the possible development of these relations. Personally, I will

go further and say that an economic basis for these relations can be put in place at any moment. . . . Concerning Hitler personally, he, too, it seems to me, given the circumstances, will not refuse to re-examine his position towards relations with Russia.[5]

One curious aspect of this quotation is Schulenburg's assertion that Litvinov, the Soviet foreign minister, was "a great supporter of Germany" and was contemplating the development of relations between the two states. Litvinov in fact pursued collective security with the West.[6] Schulenburg seems to have been trying to convince his Soviet comrade that all the essential elements for rapprochement were in place: namely, that support existed on both sides, that there was interest in mutually advantageous trade relations; and that even Hitler might be willing to modify his position, given his concerns over raw material shortages.

Did Hitler instruct Schulenburg to work toward rapprochement as early as 1937, or was the ambassador attempting to create a climate conducive to negotiations to draw Hitler into an accord with the USSR? The most probable explanation is that Hitler indeed instructed Schulenburg to maintain neutral relations, partly to gain access to raw materials, and partly to keep open the possibility of later rapprochement. The ambassador probably then acted beyond his authority in order to influence events. Regardless of Schulenburg's intentions, signs of a growing improvement in Russo-German relations continued to increase.

Rumors of a shift in relations next emerged in the summer of 1938. On June 23, Schulenburg cabled Berlin information, given him by the American chargé d'affaires in Moscow, Mr. Kirk, that reports were circulating concerning a coming German-Soviet rapprochement. A representative of the International News Service enquired at the Press Section of the People's Commissariat for Foreign Affairs (Narkomindel) to determine how Moscow would react to such an offer from Berlin. After receiving no response for two days, the reporter drafted a telegram to the press chief, Gnedin, assuming that the Soviets would reject such a move. Gnedin revised the statement to explain that any proposal by Germany for strengthening world peace would be favorably received by the Soviet government. Maintaining the standard line, Schulenburg explained to Kirk that, given ideological differences, rapprochement was impossible. Alert to a possible shift in the winds from Berlin, Schulenburg requested further information from

Weizsäcker. He considered it significant that Gnedin delayed replying to the journalist for two days and assumed that Gnedin had consulted with Litvinov prior to issuing the revision.[7]

In a separate cable to Berlin on that same day, Schulenburg described a speech Litvinov had given to his Leningrad constituency earlier that day, in which the Soviet foreign minister severely criticized the Western democracies for failing to preserve the principle of collective security. Litvinov remarked that the Soviet Union would henceforth "break with the policy of the Western Powers and decide in each case whether its own interests require co-operation with England and France."[8]

These were the signals each government extended to the other prior to the Munich agreement. After Munich, Soviet interest in reaching accord with either the Western powers or Germany intensified, as did Hitler's interest in gaining Stalin's consent for a German attack on Poland. At the 1939 New Year's Day celebrations, contrary to his usual practice, Hitler stopped to speak with Alexei Merekalov, the Soviet ambassador in Berlin, for several minutes. Hitler later bragged to his generals on August 22, 1939 that on that occasion he had initiated the pact.[9]

On New Year's Day 1939, only seven months of peace remained, and signs of a shift toward Moscow continued. Each morning German journalists attended Dr. Joseph Goebbels' press conferences held in the ministry for popular enlightenment and propaganda. The attendees were forbidden to preserve their notes, but one journalist, Carl Brammer, defied those orders.[10] According to Brammer's notes of January 25, 1939, a trade conference was to take place in Moscow at the end of the month to discuss greater machine exports from Germany to Russia and imports to Germany of Russian raw materials. In this context, political negotiations were said to be planned to ensure the Russians that the drive to the east was not real. "The Reich demands neutrality with Russia," Brammer wrote. Two days later, Brammer again recorded that talks with the Soviets were impending. Brammer remarked: "Schnurre [Dr. Karl Schnurre, German trade representative] is expected to go to Moscow and although he is not an Aryan, he has Hitler's full trust. He is recognized not just as a technical person but also as a diplomat. It is therefore probable that he will go to Moscow with general instructions to probe." If Brammer's notes accurately reflect the information issued by the regime, Hitler was likely already interested in conducting political negotiations with the Soviets by late January.

In order not to jeopardize a potential agreement with the Soviets, it was necessary to minimize publicity of any possible understanding between Germany and the West. Consequently, on February 4, Brammer noted that the rumor that Bonnet, the French foreign minister, would visit Germany was false. On February 8, press conference attendants were informed that the positive remarks that Bonnet had made concerning Germany in a recent speech should be given little publicity. On February 20, Goebbels' ministry forbade writing on the visit to Berlin by the British minister for trade. According to the official line, England believed the visit would bring much, but Germany attached little significance to it. This same line was reiterated on February 22, stressing that Germany placed no weight on the visit.

On April 1, at the christening of the *Tirpitz*, Hitler delivered an address in which he invited the Soviets to renounce the Western powers and turn toward Germany.[11] On April 17, the Soviets extended their next feeler when Ambassador Merekalov visited Weizsäcker for the first time since the Soviet ambassador assumed his post on June 5 of the previous year. In the course of their discussion over arms deliveries from the Czechoslovak Skoda works, Merekalov allegedly suggested that his country would be amenable to an improvement in relations.[12]

The extant records surrounding this encounter are contradictory. The German documents claim that the Soviets made overtures for rapprochement, while the Soviet documents suggest the opposite.[13] Based on Weizsäcker's later actions, the state secretary would have had little incentive to initiate political discussions at this time. On the other hand, the Soviet ambassador would have had reasons for alleging that the Germans had suggested an improvement in political relations. Merekalov had been intimately involved in the economic negotiations with Germany conducted several years earlier, and he may have hoped to rekindle those discussions.[14] Merekalov may also have been altering information to Litvinov on separate orders.

Stalin may have instructed Merekalov to extend a feeler to Germany without informing Litvinov that he had done so. This would explain both Merekalov's and Georgei Astakhov's (Merekalov's deputy and successor) reports back to Litvinov. Litvinov sent no written directives to the ambassador to suggest improving political relations,[15] and indeed such instructions would have been contrary to Litvinov's consistent advocacy of collective security with the West, which he had worked toward for years. This interpretation might also explain why Stalin imprisoned both Merekalov and Astakhov in Moscow, as he may have wished to conceal his actions and maintain the pretense that Germany was wooing the USSR. Stalin did, of course, imprison numerous officials, especially those who had dealings with Germany, including Radek and Kandelaki.

Based on the patterns of behavior of both the German and Soviet participants in this affair, it seems likely that the Soviets led this initiative on April 17. On that same day, Litvinov made his first overture to the British ambassador in Moscow, Sir William Seeds, initiating the triple alliance talks between Britain, France, and the Soviet Union.[16] The fact that both overtures were made on the same day suggests either that Stalin and Litvinov agreed to extend these contradictory feelers simultaneously, or that Stalin (or Merekalov and Astakhov) was acting without Litvinov's knowledge. Since the Soviet representatives in Berlin appear to have altered their reports to the foreign minister, apparently Litvinov was unaware of their initiatives.

The Nazi-Soviet pact had a definite public genesis when Stalin announced to the Party Congress on March 10, 1939 that the Soviet Union was amenable to reaching some real accord with Germany. In a striking change of tone, Stalin declared: "Britain and France have rejected the policy of collective security, of collective resistance, and have taken up a policy of non-intervention, of neutrality. . . . The policy of non-intervention means conniving at aggression, giving free rein to war."

Stalin further charged the West with attempting through their press campaigns to "poison the atmosphere and to provoke a conflict with Germany for which no visible grounds exist."[17] Perhaps Stalin's remarks merely represented a warning to the British and French, but such a generous interpretation seems unlikely, especially given that in August, during the Nazi-Soviet pact negotiations, Molotov remarked that it was in Stalin's March 10 address that he signaled to Germany his readiness to reach an accord.[18] No one in the German Embassy in Moscow could have missed such a signal, and indeed the embassy staff quickly cabled Berlin with details.

Stalin likely hoped that Hitler would respond to this overture, but his signals were predicated on the assumption that Hitler would receive them. Having made such a glaring public statement, Stalin waited. Five days later, German armies occupied Prague. The führer was marching ever closer to Poland, and Soviet neutrality, or participation, in that attack was essential to his aims.

If Hitler had truly been contemplating an agreement with Stalin—however vaguely or tentatively—he would certainly have seized upon Stalin's public overtures made in his Party Congress speech. Yet no German response resulted. Either Hitler was not interested—which seems unlikely—or he did not even know what Stalin had announced.

Stalin's removal of Litvinov on May 3 was the next signal inviting accord, and it was one which even Hitler could not miss. On May 10, Hitler assembled some of his top advisers to discuss the meaning of Litvinov's removal In attendance were Ribbentrop, General Wilhelm Keitel, Walter Hewel, Karl Schnurre, and Gustav Hilger, one of the Moscow embassy's ablest advisers. Having spent virtually the whole of his life in that country, he knew Russia, the language, culture, and politics, better than any of his peers. All who worked in the Moscow embassy deferred to him for his depth of understanding, and even occasionally referred to him as "the encyclopedia." It was a rare twist of fate that the other members of the embassy whom Hitler summoned for this critical meeting were unable to attend. Ambassador Schulenburg had to represent Germany in Persia, and General Ernst Köstring, the military attaché, was in Siberia at the time. Ribbentrop, believing Siberia to be closer to Germany than Persia (since it was part of Russia), instructed Köstring to take the next flight to Berlin. In his memoirs, Köstring remarked, "My many meetings with Ribbentrop showed ever more clearly how little ability this favorite of Hitler had for such a position of importance."[19]

Hilger had naturally heard much about the chancellor's personality over the years, but he had never met the man before this occasion. He had been forewarned that an audience with Hitler meant sitting patiently while the chancellor ranted and raved, sometimes for hours. Rarely did the invited guest have an opportunity to share his own views. Consequently, Hilger was quite surprised when the chancellor's first remark was an invitation for him to give his general impressions of the situation in the Soviet Union. Caught off guard but quick on his feet, Hilger began a lengthy review of what he saw as the most meaningful trends currently under way.

Hitler listened intently, leaning forward as Hilger spoke. When he mentioned the recent change in the foreign minister, Hitler asked Hilger

what he thought were the reasons for Litvinov's removal. Hilger replied
that he believed that Stalin had grown disenchanted with the West and was
now ready for some sort of accord with Germany. It was at this point that
Hilger discovered that Hitler had not learned of Stalin's speech to the Party
Congress. In fact, neither had Ribbentrop.

Sounding amazed, Ribbentrop asked Hilger to repeat slowly the main
segments of Stalin's speech concerning Germany. Hilger did so, yet could
scarcely believe that the foreign minister had not read the Moscow embassy's reports. Dr. Schnurre, also in attendance, corroborated Hilger's account, expressing surprise that no others present seemed to know of
Stalin's speech. Had Ribbentrop truly neglected to read these key cables,
or had he simply failed to inform Hitler about them? Was he therefore
feigning ignorance?

On March 13, the Moscow embassy wired Berlin with a substantial
review of Stalin's speech. The Foreign Ministry maintained as standard
practice log books that recorded the paths of incoming cables. Each diplomatic telegram that arrived in Berlin was noted in a log book along with
the individuals within the ministry who received copies of it. The log books
relating to this document, however, are missing. In fact, the original is also
missing; only a copy remains bearing the signatures of merely the lower
ranking officials who read that duplicate. Thus, it is impossible to establish whether Ribbentrop or Weizsäcker read the embassy's report.

But Weizsäcker at least knew of Stalin's speech by May 6, four days
before Hitler's meeting with Hilger. On May 4, the day after Litvinov was
sacked, the embassy's second in command, Kurt von Tippelskirch, cabled
Berlin regarding Litvinov's removal, asserting that the change appeared to
have resulted from differences in opinion within the Kremlin over Moscow's
pro-Western policy. Weizsäcker wrote another document of similar con-
tent. Dated May 6, 1939, the cable reiterated much of what Tippelskirch
had related, but the state secretary added a reference to Stalin's March
speech, in which the Soviet leader declared that the USSR would not be
drawn into a conflict between the capitalist nations.[20]

Weizsäcker's cable shows at the very least that he knew of Stalin's
Party Congress speech and the essence of its contents four days prior to
Hitler's meeting with Hilger. The state secretary likely had read the Moscow embassy's initial reports in March. Weizsäcker's precarious position
led him to acts of subversion ranging from dangerous leaks to tentative

silences. Although he cabled this information to various embassies, he appears to have made no effort to discuss Stalin's speech with Ribbentrop or Hitler and he surely knew that they would not read the many cables arriving daily from Moscow. The state secretary served as a conduit of information, and his silence on this point could have been one among many subtle acts of information control. His ambivalent feelings toward resistance, however, led him to lend his efforts to many of Hitler's policies.[21]

On May 26, Ribbentrop wired Schulenburg instructing him to intensify efforts at reaching agreement with the Soviets. In this cable he referred to Stalin's speech: "We recognized the change in Soviet course from Stalin's March address."[22] Of course, it was wholly unnecessary to point this out to Schulenburg, for it was his embassy that had first tried to alert Berlin to the Soviet shift. Ribbentrop appears to have been in the dark about the whole affair, and only after the meeting with Hilger did he attempt to appear informed.

Weizsäcker apparently withheld information on Stalin's speech in an effort to prevent or forestall a Nazi-Soviet rapprochement. The state secretary in fact leaked information over the likelihood of such an alliance to the British Foreign Office. Through the Kordt brothers, Weizsäcker sent word to Sir Robert Gilbert Vansittart (chief diplomatic adviser) in the hope of precluding Hitler's move.[23] The Kordts revealed that Hitler was conducting negotiations with the Soviets in order to preclude Soviet opposition to his planned attack on Poland. Erich Kordt noted:

> I learned from Hewel that Hitler said . . . that if it comes to a conclusion of an alliance between the Western Powers and the Soviet
> Union, then he would cancel the action against Poland. . . . But if
> the Western Powers embarrass themselves and go home empty-
> handed, then I can smash Poland without the danger of a conflict
> with the West.[24]

Kordt related this information to Vansittart because he, along with Weizsäcker, hoped that the British would be sufficiently disturbed by the news that they would themselves conclude an alliance with the Soviets and discourage Hitler from war.[25] The Kordts obtained Vansittart's assurances that Britain would not fail to conclude the alliance with Moscow.

Weizsäcker and the Kordt brothers were not the only ones to have

leaked information to the West regarding the coming Nazi-Soviet agreement.
A middle-level official in Germany's Moscow embassy, Hans-Heinrich
Herwarth von Bittenfeld (known to colleagues and friends simply as
"Johnny"), began in May 1939 to inform Western diplomats of nearly
every aspect of the secret negotiations occurring between Moscow and
Berlin.[26] On May 6, Herwarth first approached a friend in the Italian Embassy in Moscow, who related the information back to Rome. Herwarth's
leaks quickly found their way to Mussolini, who revealed his extensive
knowledge of the negotiations to the German ambassador in Rome,
Mackensen. Officials in the Wilhelmstraße suspected Schulenburg of
being responsible, but he was unaware of Herwarth's actions. Herwarth
felt it too risky to involve Schulenburg, not knowing how far the ambassador was prepared to go in resistance activities.[27] When it became evident
that Mussolini was not alarmed by the possibility of a Nazi-Soviet rapprochement as Herwarth had hoped, he next approached colleagues in the
British and French embassies. Before he could establish a consistent link
with those officials, the triple alliance talks assumed greater intensity, and
contact became too conspicuous. Herwarth therefore decided in mid-May to
approach the Americans.

Charles "Chip" Bohlen, an official in the American embassy in Moscow in charge of political affairs, used a dacha outside the city and often
went horseback riding near the grounds. On May 16, Herwarth rode with
Bohlen, and when they had reached a safe distance from the dacha, he informed Bohlen of the growing signs of closeness between his and the
Soviet governments. Again on May 18 he did the same, and the two continued to meet until the final days when the pact was signed. In his own
postwar memoirs, Bohlen corroborated everything Herwarth had claimed
regarding his leaks.Tto avoid being intercepted by Soviet bugging, Bohlen
wrote out his notes on his conversations with Herwarth, by hand rather
than dictating them as usual, and then encoded them for transmission directly to Secretary of State Cordell Hull. Bohlen reproduced excerpts from
his cables in his memoirs to demonstrate that he was reporting Herwarth's
precise details. When, at one point during the course of their exchanges,
Herwarth informed Bohlen that the Germans had broken off talks for the
time being, Bohlen concluded that Herwarth was not feeding him disinformation. Bohlen also noted that Hull on at least two occasions passed his

information to the British and French ambassadors in Washington, who in turn related it to their respective capitals.[28] In this way, Chamberlain came to know in considerable detail of the ongoing Nazi-Soviet negotiations.

Why did Chamberlain, who possessed numerous reports on the coming Nazi-Soviet pact from various reliable sources, fail to conclude the triple alliance talks? Chamberlain found himself under increasing domestic pressure from Churchill and others to bring the lengthy negotiations with the Soviets to a successful close. Many of the prime minister's opponents distrusted the Soviets as much as Chamberlain did, but they could see no better way to discourage further German aggression against Poland and to prevent a possible Nazi-Soviet accord. Although the general staff had a low opinion of the Red Army's strength, as it had been weakened by the purges, a political alliance with the Soviets could discourage Hitler from further aggression. By May, the general staff had completely reversed its low opinion of the Red Army, and nearly all of the prime minister's former supporters had deserted him on this issue.[29] Both Halifax and Cadogan favored the Soviet alliance. On May 20, Cadogan noted in his diary that he had come to accept the pact's necessity, but added that Chamberlain said he would resign rather than sign an alliance with the Soviets.[30] Although the Poles and Romanians refused to grant the Red Army the right to cross their territory, Britain could have ignored their objections and stepped up the discussions, if only to create the illusion that they were serious about the triple alliance. Vansittart advocated overriding Polish and Romanian objections altogether. The French pressed for the pact as well.[31]

Rather than seeking to discourage Hitler by intensifying the triple alliance talks, Chamberlain did precisely the opposite. Shortly prior to Parliament's rising, Chamberlain announced on July 31 before the House of Commons the names of the delegates he was dispatching to Moscow for military talks.[32] The prime minister could have kept secret the delegates' names for reasons of national security, but he chose instead to make the announcement public. He could have sent Lord Halifax, or his minister of defense, or any cabinet member. Instead, the delegation included not a single diplomat or soldier of influence. Rather than flying the party to Moscow, the prime minister sent them by ship to Leningrad. By selecting such low-ranking representatives, and by sending them via ship, Chamberlain made clear to the Soviets that their alliance was not desired. But the prime minister may not simply have wished to insult the Soviets. Perhaps he was also signaling to Berlin that Britain's encirclement policy of Germany had been abandoned, a cue to Berlin that peace was still possible. If Chamberlain had in fact made the offers to negotiate secretly in Switzerland through Sir Horace Wilson, as Dirksen and Wohlthat had been reporting, then this episode takes on new meaning. The prime minister's entire conduct strongly suggests that he still sought to negotiate with Hitler. Appeasement had not yet died.

By July's close, German-Soviet conversations proceeded at a quickening pace. On July 26, Dr. Schnurre dined with the Soviet chargé d'affaires, Georgei Astakhov, and Yevgeniy Barbarin, head of the Soviet trade mission, and suggested that their nations face the West together.[33] Astakhov remarked that the Soviet Union felt encircled by Germany's efforts in bringing Japan into the Anti-Comintern pact. He said that the Soviets were suspicious of German intentions, and he thought that negotiations would proceed slowly. Schnurre insisted that Germany and the USSR had no problems from the Black Sea to the Baltic that could not be solved. The Russians agreed to relate to their superiors in Moscow what had been said.

On August 3, as Wilson and Dirksen met in London, Schulenburg met with Molotov. Molotov still acted with restraint, but over the next few days, the Kremlin appeared to have reached a turning point in its decision.[34] That Moscow began a turn to German overtures shortly after the Wilson-Dirksen talks suggests that NKVD informants may have caught wind of those secret negotiations.

On August 10, the ship carrying the British and French delegates docked in Leningrad, too late to catch the night train to Moscow. The following day they traveled to Moscow, where Marshal Voroshilov presented his credentials empowering him to conclude a military alliance with the Western powers and asked his counterparts to do the same. The French official presented his authorization; the British representative could produce nothing. It was evident to Soviet leaders that Britain had no serious intentions of concluding a military alliance. The discussions that ensued bore this out. The following day Astakhov informed the Germans that the Soviet Union was now ready to resolve all outstanding differences. The decision had been reached.

As tension mounted across Europe over the Danzig question and war seemed imminent, Ribbentrop secured Stalin's consent to enter Moscow for negotiations. On August 23 the Nazi-Soviet nonaggression pact was signed, thus sealing Poland's fate and enabling World War II. Bitterly disappointed that the risks he had taken for months to convince the British and French to act had been entirely in vain, Johnny Herwarth leaked one final piece of information to his American colleague: he disclosed the details of the pact's secret protocol that divided Poland and the Baltic States among the signatories.[35] It was indeed a bitter defeat for German resistance, for the pact meant that war was now certain.

It is entirely possible that Stalin learned of the secret Anglo-German negotiations and that this information swayed his decision to ally with Hitler. One of the British meetings with German representatives became public knowledge in July 1939, when Robert Hudson's indiscretion to the press first alerted Stalin to the danger of a British stab in the back. On July 24, Ivan Maisky, the Soviet ambassador in London, wired Moscow the details of Hudson's proposals as reported in the press. Maisky, whose network of informants penetrated deep into British circles, may well have learned of the other Anglo-German conversations and alerted Stalin to the danger.

Stalin had another possible source. Captain John Herbert King, who worked as a cipher clerk in the British Foreign Office Communications Department, was one of the Soviet Union's most useful spies. Until his arrest on September 27, 1939, King was sending the USSR cables containing sensitive information from the Foreign Office, sometimes within hours of their receipt in London.[36] Either King or Maisky could have informed the Soviets of Wilson's secret talks.

But news of the Anglo-German talks could have reached Stalin through yet another means. As the Schulenburg files reveal, the NKVD had fully penetrated the German Embassy in Moscow. On July 24, Dirksen in London telegraphed Berlin of British interest in reaching accord with Germany and avoiding war. Apparently as a means of keeping embassy officials informed, Berlin sent a copy of Dirksen's cable to several embassies, Moscow among them. On August 11, the same day when British delegates met Marshal Voroshilov and revealed that they had been given no authority to form an alliance, Schulenburg received a copy of Dirksen's report, which he signed and dated. He then directed it on to the embassy's top staff—the inner circle. His deputy, Tippelskirch, and others read and signed it. At any point from the cable's receipt to its final destination within the embassy, NKVD informants might have intercepted it. If they had, Stalin would almost certainly have been notified immediately.

Stalin was already predisposed to believe that Britain and France were capable of forming a separate accord with Hitler, leaving the USSR devoid of aid.[37] If NKVD agents did intercept Dirksen's report, as they had done with so many others, this is in part what Stalin would have read:

> General ideas as to how a peaceful adjustment with Germany could be undertaken seem to have crystallized. . . . On the basis of political appeasement, which is to [e]nsure the principle of non-aggression and to achieve a delimitation of political spheres of interest by means of a comprehensive formula, a broad economic program is being worked out. . . . About these plans entertained in leading circles, State Advisor Wohlthat, who, on British initiative, had long talks about them during his stay in London last week, will be able to give more detailed information. The problem which is puzzling the sponsors of these plans most is how to start the negotiations. Public opinion is so inflamed, that if these plans of negotiations with Germany were to become public they would immediately be torpedoed by Churchill and others with the cry "No second Munich!" or "No return to appeasement!"

> . . .The persons engaged in drawing up a list of points for negotiation therefore realize that the preparatory steps vis-à-vis Germany must be shrouded in the greatest secrecy. Only when Germany's willingness to negotiate has been ascertained, and at least unanimity regarding the program, perhaps regarding certain general principles, has been attained, will the British Government feel strong enough to inform the public of its intentions and of the steps it has already taken. If it could in this way hold out the prospect of an Anglo-German adjustment, it is convinced that the public would greet the news with the greatest joy, and the obstructionists would be reduced to silence. So much is expected from the realization of this plan that it is even considered a most effective election cry, one which would assure the government parties a victory in the autumn elections, and with it the retention of power for another five years.

> . . .In conclusion, I should like to point out that the German-Polish problem has found a place in this tendency toward an adjustment with Germany, inasmuch as it is believed that in the event of an Anglo-German adjustment the solution of the Polish problem will be

easier, since a calmer atmosphere will facilitate the negotiations, and British interest in Poland will be diminished.[38]

Faced with the information contained in Dirksen's cable, and believing that the British would not hesitate to abandon the Soviet Union, Stalin would have had little choice but to sign a pact with Hitler. Stalin may have betrayed the West for fear of being betrayed himself.

The role of information flow in the Nazi-Soviet pact illuminates a curious irony that typified much of German foreign policy decision making under Hitler. Information that should have been kept secret was often common knowledge, while information that various statesmen wished to make known failed to reach their targets. Hitler had intended his negotiations with the Soviets to be clandestine, yet several diplomats leaked the news to the major European capitals. London, Paris, Rome, and Washington all had advance warnings from a variety of sources within Germany (from the Moscow embassy, the state secretary, and the chief of the Intelligence Service) that negotiations between Moscow and Berlin had been under way all summer. Conversely, Stalin's public overture to Hitler (and possibly Chamberlain's signal to the führer as well) either suffered long delays before reaching the chancellor, or they failed to make the intended impression.

These difficulties in achieving accurate, smooth information flow were not accidental. They were the result of Hitler's own leadership style and the system of confusion that his actions engendered. Both the climate of fear and the uncertainty within which the diplomats operated produced increased risk taking—risks that ultimately led to global war.

The Nazi-Soviet pact did not result from a long-range, coherent plan but rather in spite of the confused, chaotic system that governed Germany's foreign affairs. Scarcely more than three months prior to the outbreak of war, Hitler was not receiving important information regarding the shift in Soviet foreign policy. Although the final outcome might have been the same, the timing and nature of Hitler's decisions were limited by the lack of information.

Would Hitler have altered his plans to attack Poland in September 1939 if he had had all the information accurately presented to him? It is impossible to know, for consistency was not one of the chancellor's trademarks. If Hitler had known the full details of what Chamberlain was offering—if indeed Chamberlain offered to negotiate at all—then World

War II might well have taken a wholly different course. If Hitler had chosen to explore a possible agreement with Britain in the hope of obtaining her neutrality in Eastern Europe, then the Polish campaign would have been postponed at least until the spring of 1940. From this follows a chain of events about which we can only guess. Hitler might not have pursued the Nazi-Soviet pact with such urgency; the division of Eastern Europe by Soviet and German forces would then have been delayed. During the winter months, support for Churchill's policies might have grown enough to topple Chamberlain. Churchill would almost certainly have made good his proclaimed intentions to conclude the Triple Alliance pact with the French and Soviets, in which case Hitler might then have been reluctant to attack Poland. From this point, one could speculate that the World War II and even the Holocaust might never have occurred, but speculation is all it would be. For we may never know precisely what Hitler knew, nor what consequences might have ensued. The answer must forever remain in the murky realm of historical might-have-beens.

Conclusions

Information equals power in every regime. In Hitler's Reich, however, the stakes in the battle for information involved matters of life or death—and peace or war. This book has asked what Hitler and his advisers knew, how their knowledge affected policy, and why they acted as they did. In all governments, what decision makers know and how they use their knowledge are important elements of policy formation, but in Nazi Germany these questions became critical aspects of the decision-making process.

Hitler's power to make informed decisions was limited by the very system he created. Hitler trusted no one. He divulged his intentions warily, occasionally spreading disinformation to confuse his adversaries and subordinates alike. He once remarked to one of his leading generals, "You will never learn my real intentions. Not even my closest colleagues, who are convinced they know them, will ever find them out."[1] Hitler's distrustful nature spread like a poison throughout his regime, and it infected the diplomats most of all.

Beyond withholding his intentions, Hitler produced a destabilizing sense of uncertainty within the Reich by encouraging political infighting and above all by fostering a climate of fear through SS and Gestapo terror. This system led his advisers not to be cautious, but instead to take risks. They sometimes advocated perilous policies, as a means of advancing or defending their careers. And they often withheld or manipulated information, to protect their positions as well as their lives.

Hitler probably never knew how poorly information flowed within his regime or how this limited his power, even though he, himself, was part of the battle for information. The extent of the fuhrer's understanding about his government is impossible to ascertain. Despite all the documents the Nazi era bequeathed to historians, Hitler made few records of his own, and the bulk of his knowledge perished with him in the bunker. We can come closer to comprehending the riddles of the Reich, but a degree of uncertainty must always remain, for even with another century of thoughtful probing, we will never know precisely what Hitler knew. But we can determine how the chaotic flow of information limited what he knew and how it affected decision making within his regime.

Information control and the climate of fear began even as early as 1933, shaping the diplomats' dramatic support for turning Germany's eastern alliances inside out and aligning with their hated neighbor, Poland. The diplomats' decision occurred under a high degree of pressure and confusion, both from the international arena and from within the regime. Hitler's domestic anti-communist activities and openly hostile attitude toward the Soviet Union strained relations with the USSR, making a continuation of the Rapallo-era cooperation impossible. Once reports began to reach the ministry of a possible Polish-Soviet military alliance, the diplomats had to find a way of precluding Germany's encirclement. Unfortunately for the Wilhelmstraße, its decisions had to be reached while under Gestapo scrutiny following the arrest of a ministry official charged with spying for Poland. Under normal circumstances, the incident might have caused only mild consternation, but it had to be seen as part of the growing wave of Nazi terror. The state was arresting nearly 60,000 Germans within the first two years of Nazi rule, and the diplomats were trapped under the expanding net of Gestapo surveillance tactics, including the establishment of Göring's wire tapping bureau, used to record their every word. Within this context, the diplomats found themselves controlling information and supporting a risky realignment of relations, destabilizing the already shaky European balance of power.

Soon after the decision to align with Poland, the value of information became frighteningly clear. However unpleasant the Gestapo scrutiny of 1933 had been, it could only have seemed insignificant after June 30, 1934.

On that date the decision makers' environment reached a distinct turning point when the "Night of the Long Knives" finally severed the sense of security that had been fraying since the Nazi seizure of power. Most of the Reich's conservatives, save for those in the army, were caught wholly by surprise. Had Papen been forewarned, he might have been able to prevent his house arrest and the murder of his staff members. Had Neurath known what was coming, he might have been able to safeguard his ministry colleagues. Instead, they were powerless to do little more than to hope that they themselves would be spared. One lesson these men, and surely other decision makers as well, drew from this episode of state-led terror was that their ability to control information represented one of the few ways in which they could enhance their often tenuous positions, and that lack of information could prove disastrous.

With each subsequent foreign policy decision, Hitler's advisers intensified their battle over the information arsenal. Throughout his tenure as Hitler's foreign minister, Neurath continuously had to defend his precarious position against the encroachment of rivals. Both Neurath and Bülow actively and consistently sought to limit Ribbentrop's access to information to block his growing intrusions and thereby defend their own power. In the course of conducting policy, Neurath appears to have controlled information both to the chancellor, as in the Rhineland crisis, and to his ministry colleagues, as with his ostensible support for the funding of the Ethiopian military. However, Neurath's chief rival had also grasped the value of information control. Ribbentrop learned that by keeping Neurath ignorant of his activities, he could strengthen his own position and outmaneuver his immediate superior. Consequently, he obtained from Hitler the right to operate beyond the foreign minister's view, to conduct negotiations without the foreign minister's knowledge, and to report directly to the chancellor, despite Neurath's repeated attempts to prevent this scenario. Neurath's fall from power was in part the result of his failure to control the information arsenal.

Concomitant with their struggles for information control, the diplomats pursued imprudent policies, as in the case of Neurath's apparent support for the funding of the Ethiopian resistance. By pressing for this course, the foreign minister endangered Germany's clandestine rearmament program, on which Hitler's, and indeed the diplomats', revisionist plans depended. Neurath's greatest risk came during the Rhineland crisis, when he staked his career on France's unwillingness to fight. In contrast to almost unanimous opinion against the move in March 1936 from among Hitler's advisers, Neurath gambled on French weakness. If, in the process, Neurath withheld vital information from the führer—and it appears that he did—then the foreign minister took the added risk of being exposed. When his gamble paid off, it elevated him above his rivals and demonstrated to the führer that he was a man of bold action, a quality Hitler strongly favored.

By the summer of 1939, rational decision-making processes had completely broken down because of the distrust and fear that permeated Hitler's regime. Once he succeeded Neurath to the post of foreign minister, Ribbentrop also sought to control the information flow to Hitler. He successfully prevented information from reaching the führer regarding the secret Anglo-German talks of summer 1939. But Ribbentrop's immediate subordinate, State Secretary Weizsäcker, appears to have been playing the same game, withholding important information from both Ribbentrop and Hitler regarding Stalin's public overtures to Germany. Risk taking increased still further as war approached. When Weizsäcker, the Kordt brothers, and Johnny Herwarth all leaked information to the West to prevent a Nazi-Soviet rapprochement, they committed treason and thereby risked their lives. If Ambassador Dirksen, Wohlthat, and perhaps Theo Kordt as well, fabricated Chamberlain's offers to negotiate, then they took an enormous gamble on a plan with virtually no chance of success. They sought to pass their information to Hitler, but Ribbentrop thwarted them. By blocking information to Hitler—knowledge that the führer would surely have wanted. Ribbentrop risked his position as foreign minister. He then gambled that Britain would not fight, but the British were to prove him wrong.

To what extent did all this risk taking actually influence foreign policy outcomes? That risk taking hindered decision making is clear; that policy outcomes would surely have been more prudent or would have been altogether different in the absence of risk taking can never be determined. We can never know whether Hitler, if he had been in possession of all the information he desired and had not been surrounded by advisers who advocated dangerous policies, would have acted differently. What we do know, however, is that information control affected the timing and nature of his decisions, and it may even at times have altered the outcomes.

But risk taking and chaotic information flow not only affected decision making within the Third Reich, they also influenced policy outcomes in Britain and Soviet Russia, and they may have proved decisive for the outbreak of World War II. The evidence in this book suggests that Chamberlain did not abandon appeasement after Hitler's invasion of Czechoslovakia, but instead offered to discuss a nonaggression pact with Hitler on the eve of war. The German negotiators may have had incentives to exaggerate Chamberlain's proposals, but it seems that the British offers to discuss a pact through secret talks in Switzerland were in fact extended. Whether Chamberlain actually intended to forge a nonaggression pact with Germany can never be established for certain. Those who search the Public Record Office for incriminating documents are unlikely to find them, for neither Chamberlain nor Wilson would have been so foolish as to have left such records behind. How Chamberlain could have believed he could sell such a scheme to the British public or his own cabinet is unclear, unless he never intended to carry it through. If this were so, then his secret plans may have produced one of history's most stupendous backfires. The tragic irony is that even if he only hoped to entice Hitler into talks and thereby forestall a conflict, Chamberlain's place in history may sink even lower, not simply for his unwillingness to forego appeasement, but because of the unintended consequences of his actions for the outbreak of global war.

For more than half a century historians have struggled to explain Stalin's decision to ally with Hitler, but no definitive conclusion has ever emerged. This study argues that Stalin's decision to sign the Nazi-Soviet pact, which launched World War II, could well have resulted from Chamberlain's overtures to Hitler. Since the Soviet secret service had penetrated Germany's Moscow embassy, Stalin could easily have learned of Chamberlain's alleged plans for a nonaggression pact with Hitler once German Ambassador Dirksen's report from London reached the Moscow embassy. The coincidence of events—that German Ambassador Schulenburg in Moscow read Dirksen's report on August 11, 1939, and that the Soviets accepted German offers to negotiate on the following day—strongly suggests that Stalin learned of Chamberlain's alleged efforts to conclude a separate pact with Hitler. If this did occur, then Stalin's decision takes on a new dimension. Already predisposed to believe that the British would sell him out, his decision may have resulted not solely from a desire to betray the West or to destroy Poland, but also out of fear of being betrayed himself.

The debates surrounding Nazi Germany continue, but central to them all is the question of how decisions were reached. Whether considering decision making with respect to the Holocaust, the German resistance, Hitler's expansionist aims, or other contentious issues, future studies may benefit from an analysis of the role of environment and information flow as key factors in policy formation. The findings of this work may also have relevance for similar studies of comparable dictatorships. Within Hitler's violent regime, the decision maker's environment profoundly shaped his behavior. Within other regimes where fear, confusion, and uncertainty reign, such as Stalin's Russia, Pinochet's Chile, or contemporary Burma, Syria, North Korea, and Iraq, chaotic information flow and advocacy of risky policies may also become features of those nations' decision-making processes and may have serious implications for foreign policy making. Despite ample indications of American intentions before the Gulf War, Saddam Hussein chose a policy of enormous risk, one that resulted in destruction and defeat. Was his decision based on his own irrational calculations, a desire to combat the United States no matter the cost, or could it have come in part from the information his advisers brought him and the climate of fear within which they function? And if fear, information control, and risk are in fact salient aspects of Saddam's regime, what impact can U.S. policy makers expect their signals to have in future confrontations with Iraq?

Any study of Nazi Germany must confront the question: why would good people support a bad regime? Why did Bernhard von Bülow take the trouble of drafting a resignation letter and then fail to submit it? What led men like Neurath and Papen to serve the regime, while Herwarth and Schulenburg tried to sabotage it? This book has sought to help us comprehend why these men acted as they did by conveying the context within which they had to function.

What if you had been one of Hitler's diplomats. How would you have reacted each day at work, surrounded by subtle terror and the omnipresent threat of violence? On the surface, you raised the Nazi salute and hailed the Party's success. But in the darker world, the one in which you lived under Gestapo surveillance, you had to struggle to survive. Each day you knew that your phones were tapped, your words recorded, your correspondence penetrated, and your actions observed. You witnessed your government abolish civil liberties, destroy parliamentary democracy, and strangle freedom of thought. And if you harbored any hopes of preserving your personal safety, those hopes were shattered when your government murdered your colleagues in a sudden burst of terror. Each day thereafter you defended your position from the Party rivals who aimed to push you out. All the while you struggled to glean your boss's will, but he never shared it with you. In that world, information equaled more than power. You battled for information not just to protect and advance your career but to safeguard your life. And you gambled when you had to for the same reasons, even if it meant you might help ignite total war.

Each of the men who played a leading part in influencing Germany's foreign policy throughout the prewar decade suffered under the climate of fear, and while all of them engaged in information control and risk taking, each chose a different course toward degrees of resistance or support. Human motivations are rarely clear-cut. No gene for risk taking can fully explain it, and no grand unifying theory can predict how each individual will react. We can only ask what led them all to take such risks. Within such an uncertain environment, why were the decision makers not cowed into submission? Some must have hoped to advance their careers by pressing for bold actions, since this is what Hitler favored. Others, who might have been more circumspect in a less stable setting, felt compelled to act boldly, not to advance their careers, but to avoid being removed from power. Some risked their lives to control information, believing it necessary just to stay alive. And others risked their lives to prevent a war. All were responding to the climate of fear. Whatever the individual motivations were, risk taking was high because the stakes were so high, and playing it safe seemed a losing prospect. Whether they sought to avert a war or to launch one, to advance their careers or prevent removal, to undercut rivals or defend themselves, the decision makers understood that within such a frenetic environment, maintaining the status quo accomplished nothing. Risk taking and information control were essential for survival or success in Hitler's darker world.

After the war at the International Military Tribunal in Nuremberg, Ribbentrop was found guilty of crimes against humanity and hanged. The aging Neurath, though sentenced to prison, was released early on grounds of ill health. The once German chancellor, Franz von Papen, who had narrowly escaped Hitler's first purge and avoided dismissal before the Austrian annexation, proved his survival skills as remarkably after the war as he had done when serving the Reich. Though convicted as a Nazi Party leader, he was later released on appeal. He published his memoirs and died in 1969 at the considerable age of ninety. Herbert von Dirksen, the artful diplomat who seemed ever in the right post at the right time, was forced to flee his estate at Groeditzberg as the Soviet Red army advanced on Berlin.

Dirksen was found not guilty at Nuremberg, and after publishing his memoirs, he died in 1955. Ambassador Count Friedrich Werner von der Schulenburg, who had sought to improve German-Soviet relations, was hanged by the Nazis for his part in the July 1944 plot to assassinate the führer. But his colleague in the Moscow embassy, Johnny Herwarth, who had worked against the Nazi-Soviet pact, joined a cavalry division and fought for his country. As for Hitler's state secretary, Ernst von Weizsäcker, he was sentenced to prison, but was later released and died soon thereafter. His son, Richard, a gifted lawyer who defended his father before the tribunal, went on to enjoy a brilliant career and eventually served for a decade as Germany's president when the Berlin wall came down and the nation re-united.

Unlike his advisers, Hitler's own apocalyptic end, committing suicide by poison and having his body burned, cheated both the hangman and historian alike. He robbed one of justice and the other of a final chance to learn more of what Hitler really knew. Yet despite all he managed to dissemble and destroy, he could not prevent us from discerning the environment in which he was constrained. Although Hitler is ultimately responsible for the actions of his Reich, he was not the absolute master of the decision-making process. In the frenzied atmosphere of Hitler's Reich, where neither one's career nor one's life was secure, Hitler's power to make informed decisions was limited by the confused, frenetic system which he himself created.

Notes

Hitler's Opening Gambit

1. Robert Gellately, *Backing Hitler: Consent and Coercion in Nazi Germany* (New York: Oxford University Press, 2001), p. 256.

2. Eric A. Johnson, *Nazi Terror: The Gestapo, Jews, and Ordinary Germans* (New York: Basic Books, 1999), p. 161-162.

3. Johnson, *Nazi Terror*, p. 162.

4. Viktor Klemperer, *I Will Bear Witness: A Diary of the Nazi Years* (New York: Random House, 1998–1999), p. 7.

5. Klemperer, *I Will*, p. 17.

6. Peter Krüger, "Struktur, Organization, und Außenpolitische Wirkungsmöglichkeiten der Leitenden Beamten des Auswärtigen Dienstes, 1921–1933," pp. 101–169, in Klaus Schwabe, ed., *Das Diplomatische Korps, 1871–1945* (Boppard am Rhein: Harald Boldt, 1985), pp. 102–103.

7. Christoph Kimmich, *German Foreign Policy 1918–45: A Guide to Research and Research Materials* (Wilmington: Scholarly Research, 1991), p. 3.

8. Krüger, "Struktur," p. 107.

9. For more on Rosenberg's activities within the party, see Robert Cecil, *The Myth of the Master Race: Alfred Rosenberg and Nazi Ideology* (Birkenhead: Willner Brothers, 1972), especially ch. 2.

10. Erich Kordt, *Nicht aus den Akten . . . Die Wilhelmstraße in Frieden und Krieg, Erlebnisse, Begegnungen, und Eindrücke, 1928–1945* (Stuttgart: Union Deutsche, 1950), pp. 73–74.

11. For more on Göring's activities see David Irving, *Breach of Security:*

The German Secret Intelligence File on Events Leading to the Second World War (London: William Kimber and Co, 1968); and John Heineman, *Hitler's First Foreign Minister: Constantin Freiherr von Neurath, Diplomat and Statesman* (Berkeley: Univ. of California Press, 1979), p. 119.

12. Hans-Adolf Jacobsen, *Nationalsozialistische Außenpolitik, 1933–1938* (Frankfurt: Metzner, 1968). p. 133.

13. Gerhard L. Weinberg, ed., *Hitler's Secret Book* (New York: Grove Press, 1961), p. 140.

14. Weinberg, *Secret Book*, pp. 47–48.

15. Weinberg, *Secret Book*, pp. 149–151.

16. Results of the 1931 census revealed that based on linguistic criteria Ukrainians constituted 13.9% of Poland's total population, Yiddish-speaking Jews constituted 8.7%, and Byelorussians were 3.1%. Germans made up only 2.3%. Cited in Norman Davies, *God's Playground* (Oxford: Clarendon Press, 1981), p. 404.

17. See, for example, Hans Gatzke, *Stresemann and the Rearmament of Germany* (Baltimore: Johns Hopkins University Press, 1954).

18. Gerald Freund, *Unholy Alliance: Russian-German Relations from the Treaty of Brest-Litovsk to the Treaty of Berlin* (London: Chatto and Windus, 1957), p. 118.

19. G. M. Gathorne-Hardy, *A Short History of International Affairs, 1920–1939* (London: Oxford University Press, 1950), p. 103.

20. Freund, *Unholy Alliance*, pp. 84–85.

21. F. L. Carsten, *Reichswehr and Politics, 1919–1933* (Cologne: Kipenheuer and Witsch, 1964), p. 140.

22. PA, R 30718 K/15. Geheimakten (secret files) regarding political relations with Poland, 1 August 1930–31 July 1933. 19 Jan. 1933. Aufz. von Bülow.

23. PA, 8 Feb. 1933. Aufz. von Bibenstein.

24. Christope Kimmich, *The Free City: Danzig and German Foreign Policy, 1919–1934* (New Haven, CT: Yale Univ. Press), p. 137.

25. Kimmich, *Free City*, p. 137.

26. Kimmich, *Free City*, p. 98.

27. PA R 30718 K/15. 12 April 1933. Aufz. Martius to Foreign Ministry leaders.

28. PA, Aufz. on Polish war industries. The date and signature are unclear, but the report appears to have been sent in the same month as other similar cables on Polish war preparations.

29. PA, Nachlaß Aschmann, pp. 51–52. 20 April 1933. Stoiko Information, Nr. 316.

30. *ADAP*, C/II, p. 323. Hassell to AA.

31. PA R 30718K/15. 24 April 1933. Bülow to Blomberg.

32. PA, R 30718 K/15. 25 and 29 April 1933. Moltke to AA.

33. PA, R 30719 K/16. 25 April 1933. Koch to AA.

34. PA, R 30718 K/15. Labeled "secret," this cable on Polish war plans contains no identifiable signature.

35. PA, R 30759/2/13. 29 April 1933. Moltke to AA.

36. *ADAP*, C/I, p. 363. The Polish documents record a different tone. Ambassador Wysocki informed Beck that Hitler's tone was genial and accommodating. Telegram Wysocki to Beck, 2 May 1933. Polish Ministry for Foreign Affairs, *Polish White Book, Official Documents Concerning Polish-German and Polish-Soviet Relations, 1933—1939* (New York: Roy Publishers), pp. 11—13.

37. PA R 30718 K/15. 12 May 1933. Aufz. Bibenstein.

38. PA, R 30759/2/6. 8 May 1933. Meyer to Dirksen.

39. PA, R 30759/2/8. 14 May 1933. Dirksen to AA.

40. PA, R 30759/2/9. 15 May 1933. Bülow to ambassadors in Paris and Bucharest.

41. Herbert von Dirksen, *Moskau-Tokio-London* (Stuttgart: W. Kohlhammer Verlag, 1949), p. 123.

42. BA BL, Handakten von Neurath, 0901/60966/1-30. Denkschrift von Bülow. 13 March 1933.

43. PA, Nachlaß Lieeres von Wilkau, Band 3.

44. PA, R 29488. Bülow's resignation letter was first discovered by Peter Krüger and analyzed in Krüger and Hahn, "Loyalitätskonflikt."

45. Wilhelm Deist and others, eds., *Das Deutsche Reich und der Zweite Weltkrieg*, vol. I (Stuttgart: Deutsche Verlags-Anstalt, 1979), pp. 566—569.

46. *Polish White Book*, pp. 15—16. 13 July 1933. Wysocki to Beck.

47. PA, R 30095 A, I/1/41. Schindler to AA and Reichswehrministerium. 19 July 1933. All of the military attaché files used in this chapter are drawn from the Brandakten, records that were severely damaged by fire and that only recently have been restored after meticulous efforts by foreign ministry archivists.

48. PA, I/1/42.

49. PA, I/1/50-52. Schindler to AA and Reichswehrministerium. 3 August 1933.

50. PA, R 30759/2/19-20. 5 September 1933.

51. PA, R 81472/40/98. 8 Sept. 1933. Leitner to foreign minister.

52. BA K, ZSg. 101 Brammer. Band 1, p. 100.

53. PA, Nachlaß Lieeres von Wilkau. 12 September 1933. Meyer to Bülow.

54. PA, R 30095 I/1/93-96. Militärattaché Warschau. 20 Sept. 1933. Schindler to AA and Reichswehrministerium.

55. *ADAP*, C/II, pp. 829—830.

56. Foreign Ministry records refer to Hahn as "Leiter der Telegraph Union" and no Christian name is specified. His exact occupation is unclear.

57. PA, R 81473/41—42. 5 Oct. 1933. Aufz. Hahn over talks with Beck.

58. *ADAP*, C-III, p. 60. 1 Nov. 1933. Aufz. Meyer.

59. Edward W. Bennett, *German Rearmament and the West, 1932—1933*

(Princeton, NJ: Princeton University Press, 1979), pp. 488–490. See also Wilhelm Deist, *The Wehrmacht and German Rearmament* (Toronto: University of Toronto Press, 1981), pp. 28–35.

60. Kimmich, *Free City*, p. 148.

61. Kimmich, *Free City*, p. 149.

62. *Polish White Book*, pp. 16–19. 15 November 1933. Lipski to Beck.

63. Bennett, *German Rearmament*, pp. 496–497. Bennett dated Hitler's instructions to build troop strength at sometime between 30 November and 9 December 1933.

64. *Polish White Book*, pp. 20–21.

65. Kimmich, *Free City*, p. 151. Cited from Hermann Rauschning, *Hitler Speaks*, p. 123.

66. BA BL, R 0901-60966/1/25. Handakten Neurath, Allgemeine Außenpolitik.

67. Adolf Hitler, *Mein Kampf* (New York: Reynal & Hitchcock, 1939), p. 959. Edition published by arrangement with Houghton Mifflin Co., Boston, Mass. He reiterated this view in his unpublished second book. Weinberg, *Secret Book*, p. 134.

68. PA, R 30747/E463735. 19 Feb. 1934. Moltke to AA.

69. PA, R 30748/II. Unsigned Aufz. 23 March 1934.

The Longest Knife

1. Robert Gellately, *The Gestapo and German Society: Enforcing Racial Policy, 1933–1945* (Oxford: Clarendon Press, 1990), p. 10.

2. John W. Wheeler-Bennett, *The Nemesis of Power: The German Army in Politics, 1918–1945* (London: MacMillan, 1953), p. 323.

3. Martin Gilbert, *The Holocaust: The Jewish Tragedy* (London: Collins, 1986), p. 44.

4. The sheer volume of papers that comprise the foreign minister's *Handakten* (official directives) is overwhelming. From the chief diplomat down, the documentation of events is by any reasonable measure exceptional. Beyond official memoranda and reports, the diplomats' written remains often include their love letters and poems to wives, private letters between old friends, congratulatory birthday wishes, postcards sent by friends and colleagues from vacation spots, travelogues detailing impressions from their journeys, diary entries, menus from favorite restaurants, bills from dry cleaners, and so on. One key diplomat's personal papers even include letters from his Danish mistress, who less than subtly sought to extort diamond jewelry and fur coats from him. Another diplomat's records contain the draft of a play he had written parodying his superiors and their eccentricities.

5. There were, of course, a few German officials, such as Admiral Canaris, who did make records of their resistance, and these documents often proved incriminating after the assassination attempt on Hitler in 1944.

6. Johnson, *Nazi Terror*, p. 169.

7. Robert O'Neill, *The German Army and the Nazi Party, 1933–1939*
(London: Cassell, 1966), p. 35.

8. Ivone Kirkpatrick, *The Inner Circle: Memoirs of Ivone Kirkpatrick*
(London: MacMillan, 1959), p. 53.

9. Kirkpatrick, *Inner Circle*, p. 53.

10. O'Neill, *German Army*, p. 38.

11. O'Neill, *German Army*, pp. 41–42.

12. O'Neill, *German Army*, p. 45.

13. O'Neill, *German Army*, pp. 46–47. See also Nicholas Reynolds, *Treason Was No Crime: Ludwig Beck, Chief of the German General Staff* (London: William Kimber, 1976), p. 51.

14. For a personal account of Papen's intentions as divulged to a close observer, see Sir John Wheeler-Bennett, *Knaves, Fools, and Heroes: Europe Between the Wars* (London: MacMillan, 1974), pp. 88–92.

15. Ian Kershaw, *The Hitler Myth: Image and Reality in the Third Reich* (Oxford: Oxford Univ. Press, 1987), p. 509.

16. Franz von Papen, *Memoirs* (London: Andre Deutsch, 1952), pp. 311–312. According to Papen's account, many cried, "Heil Marburg!" Although Papen's memoirs represent an undeniable attempt to rehabilitate his reputation, they cannot be dismissed altogether. In this particular instance, the memoirs (which were published three years prior to Papen's) of the French ambassador in Berlin, François-Poncet, corroborate the deputy chancellor's account. See André François-Poncet, *The Fateful Years: Memoirs of a French Ambassador in Berlin, 1931–1938* (New York: Harcourt, Brace, 1949), pp. 131–332. See also Karl Vincent Krogmann, *Es Ging um Deutschlands Zukunft* (Landsberg: Landsberger Verlag-Anstalt, 1976), pp. 145–147.

17. Kershaw, *Hitler*, p. 510.

18. Kershaw, p. 510.

19. Kershaw, *Hitler*, p. 512.

20. Kershaw, p. 514.

21. Dietrich Orlow, *The History of the Nazi Party: Volume II, 1933–1945* (Pittsburgh: Univ. of Pittsburgh Press, 1973), p. 119. To support the view that Hitler tolerated only Hess's company, Orlow cited the sometimes unreliable source, Hermann Rauschning, *Hitler Speaks* (London, 1938), p. 171.

22. See K. D. Bracher, *Die Nationalsozialistische Machtergreifung: Studien zur Errichtung des totalitären Herrschaftssystem in Deutschland* (Frankfurt am Main: Ullstein, 1974), iii, p. 359, and Hermann Mau, "Die 'Zweiter Revolution' —der 30. Juni 1934," *VfZ*, p. 134.

23. A similar point is made by Robert Gellately in Gellately, *Gestapo*, p. 43.

24. Elke Fröhlich, ed., *Die Tagebücher von Joseph Goebbels: Teil I, Aufzeichnungen, 1924–1941* (Munich: K. G. Sauer, 1987), p. 473, 29 June 1934.

25. Papen, *Memoirs*, pp. 314–318.

26. Franz von Papen, "Rede des Vizekanzlers von Papen vor dem Universitätsbund, Marburg. 17. Juni 1934," (Berlin: Germania, 1934), p. 14.

27. William E. Dodd Jr. and Martha Dodd, eds., *Ambassador Dodd's Diary* (New York, 1941), pp. 117–120.

28. Gunnar Hagglof, *Diplomat: Memoirs of a Swedish Envoy* (London: The Bodley Head, 1972), pp. 94–95.

29. Hagglof, *Diplomat*, pp. 94–95.

30. Hagglof, *Diplomat*, p. 189.

31. Bella Fromm, *Blood and Banquets: A Berlin Social Diary* (London: Geoffrey Bles, 1942), p. 151.

32. Fromm, *Blood*, p. 153.

33. Fromm, *Blood*, p. 153.

34. Fromm, *Blood*, p. 154.

35. Lutz Graf Schwerin von Krosigk, *Es Geschah in Deutschland: Menschenbilder unseres Jahrhunderts* (Tübingen: Reiner Wunderlich Verlag, Herman Leinns, 1951), pp. 205–207. Krosigk's remarks do not lend themselves readily to translation. The final two sentences of the original text cited read: "An diesem Tage wurden die Dämme der Rechtssicherheit eingerissen. Von da an waren Gut und Blut der Deutschen dem Fanatismus, der Willkür, ja oft auch dem widrigen Zufall schutzlos preisgegeben."

36. François-Poncet, *Fateful Years*, p. 133.

37. Kirkpatrick, *Inner Circle*, pp. 56–57.

38. Kirkpatrick, *Inner Circle*, pp. 56–57.

39. Charlotte Beradt, *Third Reich of Dreams: Nightmares of a Nation, 1933–1939* (Northhamptonshire: Aquarian Press, 1985), p. 37. First published in 1966 as *Das Dritte Reich des Traums*.

40. Beradt, *Dreams*, pp. 45–47.

Risk in the Rhineland

1. Kimmich, *German Foreign Policy*, p. 19.

2. BA BL, R 901/60967/82-83, "Aufzeichnungen über politische Gespräche, Jan. 1935–Jan. 1938," *Handakten von Neurath*. This document may have escaped attention because it never appeared in the published documentary collections, *Documents on German Foreign Policy, 1918–1945*. Neurath's *Handakten* were previously held in the East German State Archives and were transferred only in 1996 to Berlin Lichterfelde.

3. *DGFP*, C/IV, p. 916. Köster to Berlin.

4. BA BL, 0901/60974/37-38, 19 March 1935.

5. BA BL, 0901/60974/39-49, 4 November 1935. Neurath to Köpke.

6. For one clear example of their territorial squabbling, see BA BL, 0901/60974/56-70, 20 February 1936.

7. BA BL, R 901/60975/47-48, 5 July 1934.

8. BA BL, R 901/60975/71, 17 November 1934. Neurath to Hitler.

9. BA BL, R 901/60975/81-83, 19 January 1935.

10. BA BL, R 901/60975/84-86, 27 May 1935.

11. BA BL, R 901/60975/87, 29 May 1935.

12. Stephen A. Schuker, "France and the Remilitarization of the Rhineland, 1936," *French Historical Studies* (1986), pp. 299–337. See also Alan Bullock, *Hitler and Stalin: Parallel Lives* (London: HarperCollins, 1993), p. 569. "The French documents leave no doubt that, despite the warnings they received, neither the French government . . . nor the French officials and General Staff, were able to draw up a plan to deal with either possibility." The possibilities to which Bullock is referring are a rupture with Italy over oil sanctions and Hitler's expected remilitarization of the Rhine.

13. Schuker, "France and the Remilitarization," p. 318.

14. James Thomas Emmerson, *The Rhineland Crisis, 7 March 1936: A Study in Multilateral Diplomacy* (London: 1977), p. 77.

15. See Emmerson, *Rhineland Crisis*, p. 77. Emmerson wrote: "Nevertheless, neither Hitler nor Neurath nor Forster believed the French would react violently to a coup, so long as it was not and could not be seen as a preparation for an attack on France. Their confidence stemmed from their knowledge of French domestic weakness, and from the convinction that Paris would not march without Britain, whose desire for a military solution was deemed non-existent." Among the printed documents Emmerson cited to support the assertion that Neurath and Hitler believed that France would not fight, he relied on *DGFP*, C/IV, p. 1142 and p. 1164, the two Hassell memoranda that will be discussed later and that show only the ambassador's impression of Neurath's views. For the claim that their confidence stemmed from a knowledge of French weakness and British unwillingness to fight, he cited *DGFP*, C/IV, p. 1034, Hassell's report of the Italian undersecretary of state's opinion of French attitudes; p. 1044, Hassell's report that Mussolini said that Flandin was at heart opposed to war. See also pp. 859, 916, 925, 974, 1042, 1112-3. Forster to Berlin. 7 Feb. 1936.

16. Kershaw, *Hitler*, p. 581.

17. BA K, *Kleine Erwerbung* Nr. 903. NKVD files on Ambassador Schulenburg, 15 January 1936.

18. Kershaw, *Hitler*, p. 586.

19. Nicholas Reynolds, *Treason Was No Crime: Ludwig Beck, Chief of the German General Staff* (London: William Kimber, 1976), p. 108.

20. Reynolds, *Treason*, p. 107.

21. Klaus-Jürgen Müller, *General Ludwig Beck: Studien und Dokumente zur politisch-militärisch Vorstellungswelt und Tätigkeit des Generalstabschefs des deutschen Heeres, 1933–1938* (Boppard am Rhein: 1980), p. 216.

22. PA, R 30075. Militärattaché Paris, 9 Jan. 1936.

23. PA, R 30079/37-42. Luftattaché Paris. 20 Feb. 1936. Kühlenthal to AA and Reichswehrministerium.

24. Reynolds, *Treason*, p. 109.

25. Reynolds, *Treason*, p. 109.

26. Wachlav Jedrzejewicz, ed., *Diplomat in Berlin, 1933–1939: Papers and Memoirs of Jozef Lipski* (New York: 1968), p. 252.

27. *DGFP*, C/IV, p. 1166.

28. *DGFP*, C/IV, p. 1173. Hassell memorandum, 22 Feb. 1936.

29. Elke Fröhlich, *Die Tagebücher von Joseph Goebbels: Teil I, Aufzeichnungen 1924-1941* (Munich: K. G. Saur, 1987), p. 576.

30. Fröhlich, *Tagebücher*, p. 577.

31. Frölich, *Tagebücher*, pp. 577–581. See entries on 2, 4, 6, and 8 March.

32. Paul Schmidt, *Statist auf diplomatischer Bühne* (Bonn: 1949), p. 320. The translation above is from Bullock, *Hitler and Stalin*, p. 570. The phrase "with our tail between our legs" is perhaps more literally and accurately rendered "cursing and in shame."

33. Kershaw, *Hitler*, pp. 584–585.

34. To support the assertion of Neurath's caution and Ribbentrop's encouragement, Kershaw cited Funke, "7. März 1936," pp. 279–282; Heinz Höhne, *Die Zeit der Illusionen, Hitler und die Anfänge des 3. Reiches 1933 bis 1936* (Düsseldorf: 1991), pp. 323–324; Robertson, "Zur Wiederbesetzung", pp. 192, 194–196, 203–204; and *DGFP*, C/IV, pp. 1164–1166. The Funke article demonstrates Hitler's wavering, not his strong conviction. Höhne's conclusions regarding Neurath's caution are based on the Hassell memorandum of February 19. The Robertson article is mostly a collection of documents from the series *DGFP*, and the pages cited refer to Hassell's memoranda. The first of these is his February 14 report that will be discussed later and that does not show either Neurath's caution or Ribbentrop's encouragement; Hassell merely mentions that Hitler discussed with those men (along with Göring, Blomberg, and Fritsch) the possibility of using the Franco-Soviet pact as a pretext for remilitarization. The second is the February 19 memorandum described in this section. The last is from February 23, regarding his meeting with Neurath, Hitler, and Ribbentrop. This shows Hassell's impression that Ribbentrop egged Hitler onward, and it reiterates that Neurath had expressed serious reservations to him. However, it also reveals Hassell's consternation over Neurath's behavior.

35. *DGFP*, C/IV, pp. 1163–1166.

36. These two men were clearly not of like mind regarding Hitler and his agenda, as evidenced by Hassell's participation in the assassination attempt on the chancellor in 1944 and his subsequent execution.

37. *Trial of the Major War Criminals* (hereafter TMWC), German Edition (Nuremberg, 1947), 10, pp. 247–248.

38. *DGFP*, C/IV, p. 917. Attempting to support his claim that Neurath was the prime initiator of remilitarization, Heineman alleged that while Neurath told Phipps that the demilitarized zone would come to an end, Hitler remained silent. See Heineman, *Hitler's First Foreign Minister*, p. 112. But Heineman cited only Neurath's memorandum as evidence. The fact that Neurath did not mention Hitler's comments at this point cannot be seen as evidence that Hitler made none.

39. *DGFP*, C/IV, p. 917.

40. BA BL, RM 40/52-53. *Neurath Denkschrift*. 17 January 1936.

41. TMWC, XVII, pp. 50–51.

42. See Max Braubach, *Der Einmarsch deutsche Truppen in die entmilitarisierte Zone am Rhein in März 1936: Ein Beitrag zur Vorgeschichte des Zweiten Weltkrieges* (Cologne: 1956), pp. 13–14.

43. *DGFP*, C/IV, p. 1142. Hassell memorandum, officially dated February 14, 1936.

44. Fröhlich, *Tagebücher*, pp. 576–577. 28 Feb.:"*Der Führer ist noch unschlüssig.*" 1 March: "*Frage Rheinland. Noch kein Entschluß.*"

45. Manfred Funke asserted that Hitler's wavering and uncertainty is evidenced by his vacillating statements. Funke argued that Hitler contradicted himself by declaring on one occasion that France would not fight, but at other times expressing his concerns. Funke concluded that "for Hitler the question whether France would retaliate with military measures over the nullification of the demilitarized zone was entirely open." Funke, "7. März 1936.Fall zum außenpolitischen Führungsstil Hitlers," in Wolfgang Michalka (ed.), *Nationalsozialistische Außenpolitik* (Darmstadt: 1978) p. 288.

46. BA BL, R 901/60967/117-23, 20 January 1936.

47. Gregor Schöllgen, *A Conservative against Hitler: Ulrich von Hassell: Diplomat in Imperial Germany, The Weimar Republic, and the Third Reich, 1881–1944* (London: 1991), pp. 55-57, and Hans-Adolf Jacobsen, *Nationalsozialistische Außenpolitik, 1933–1938* (Frankfurt am Main: 1968), pp. 348, 368.

48. *DGFP*, C/IV, p. 1142.

49. Bullock, *Hitler and Stalin*, p. 570.

50. Fröhlich, *Tagebücher*, p. 578. 4 March 1936.

51. See Bullock, *Hitler and Stalin*, p. 571. On Blomberg's call for withdrawal, see Kershaw, *Hitler*, p. 589. On Hitler's nerves see Schmidt, *Nicht aus den Akten*, pp. 134–135. Schmidt recorded that two years after the event a ministry official was released from duty for having said that on March 7 the foreign minister was more courageous than Hitler.

52. PA Bonn, R 28822/88, 27 March 1936.

53. BA BL, NS 10: *Persönlicher Adjutant des Führers*, 28 March 1936.

54. BA BL, NS 10: *Persönlicher*.

55. Klemperer, *I Will Bear Witness*, p. 156.

Raising the Stakes

1. Dennis Mack Smith, *Mussolini's Roman Empire* (London: Longman, 1976), p. 65.

2. *ADAP*, C, p. 527.

3. *ADAP*, C, p. 741.

4. *ADAP*, C, p. 742.

5. *ADAP*, C, p. 145.

6. This appears to have been less true within Britain. The Ethiopian gov-

ernment had also sought to procure loans and weapons from Britain, but this proved somewhat more difficult. One estimate of Ethiopian strength showed that its army possessed a mere 50 to 60 thousand rifles and 600 to 800 machine guns, but with very limited ammunition. Although the Solley Armament Company was prepared to sell the Ethiopians enough rifles and ammunition to double or triple their stocks, Vansittart prohibited the sale. It was feared that if these arms should be captured and their English markings discovered, it would appear that Britain was sponsoring the Ethiopian resistance. While Vansittart's decision was based on prudent assessment of Britain's relations on the continent, the international embargo imposed on 12 October made it exceedingly difficult for the Ethiopians to arm themselves. See George W. Bear, *Test Case: Italy, Ethiopia, and the League of Nations* (Stanford: Hoover Institution Press, 1976), pp. 79–80.

7. Hitler, *Mein Kampf*, vol. 2, ch. 13.

8. *DGFP*, C/IV, pp. 347–348.

9. *ADAP*, C/IV, pp. 446–447, fn. 3. According to the printed documents, no reply from Neurath to Bülow's telegram was found.

10. Heineman, *Hitler's First Foreign Minister*, p. 108.

11. BA Koblenz, Nachlaß von Neurath. 20 July 1935. One reason why this document has not hitherto been analyzed may be because it did not appear in either the published records (*DGFP*) or in either of the two principal collections of Neurath's papers, his Handakten in Berlin and his other official papers in Bonn. The Koblenz Nachlaß contains a mere hodgepodge of miscellaneous documents.

12. BA Koblenz, 20 July 1935.

13. BA Koblenz, Nachlaß von Neurath. Bülow to Neurath. 3 August 1935.

14. BA Koblenz, 3 August 1935.

15. A review of the other documents that Heineman cited to support his claim that Neurath sought neutrality reveals little substantial evidence. Those documents show mostly what Neurath told the Italian ambassador and other foreign representatives. Heineman cited *DGFP*, C/IV, pp. 563–565, an August 19 memorandum from Bülow who told the Italian ambassador that Germany wanted nothing to do with the Italo-Abyssinian conflict and Neurath wrote in the margin, "Quite correct"; pp. 693–695, a memorandum from Köpke showing that Italian Ambassador Attolico believed the führer supported German neutrality based on his Sept. 15 Reichstag speech (which actually referred to German neutrality over Memel and Lithuania); pp. 703704, shows foreign ministry official Kotze's report that Neurath told Hitler by phone to state in a public speech that Germany sought neutrality in the conflict; p. 728, an Oct. 12 memorandum from Neurath stating that he informed Attolico that Germany was neutral; pp. 776–777, a memorandum from Meissner on Oct. 25 recording that Hitler told the retiring Belgian minister in Berlin that "we were indeed in no way involved and completely neutral"; pp. 794–796, shows how Krauel, the German consul in Geneva, told the League's Transit Sub-Committee that Germany was neutral; pp. 798–799, a memorandum from Bülow in which Krauel told League representatives that "we had no intention of deriving any special opportunistic profit from the present situation."

16. *DGFP*, C/IV, pp. 347–348. Neurath to Hassell. 24 June 1935.

18. Hassell consistently sought closer Italo-German relations. For one clear example, see *DGFP*, C/IV, pp. 417–419. Hassell to foreign ministry. 5 July 1935.

19. According to Dennis Mack Smith, Mussolini possessed such an "uncontrollable passion for secret material" that his ministers sometimes tried to get information to him by working it into private telephone conversations which they knew he was tapping. *Mussolini's Roman Empire*, p. 69.

20. *DGFP*, C/IV, p. 727.

21. *DGFP*, C/IV, pp. 803–804.

23. PA, R 106422. "Handel mit Kriegsgeräte—Europa, 1936. Aufz. Schmieden. 26 July 1936.

24. PA, R 30035 K, "*Aus- und Einfuhr von Kriegsgeräte nach Osteuropaische Länder, 1935-1936,*" 28 Jan. 1936. Ethiopian consul general to Prüfer.

25. PA, R 30035 K, 11 March 1936. The official's signature is illegible.

26. Mack Smith, *Mussolini's Roman Empire*, pp. 73–74. Smith detailed the Italian campaigns and noted that a "fascist British general" commented in the *Daily Mail* that the fine spray of mustard gas had proved decisive in Italy's success.

27. Heineman, *Hitler's First Foreign Minister*, pp. 126–127. Upon Ribbentrop's appointment as ambassador, Neurath allegedly remarked, "Ribbentrop will soon discover that it is easier to have compliments paid to one as a representative of a brand of champagne than as representative of the government of the Reich."

28. Kordt, *Nicht aus den Akten*, p. 79.

29. Kordt, *Nicht aus den Akten*, p. 79.

30. Kordt, *Nicht aus den Akten*, p. 79.

31. Heineman, *Hitler's First Foreign Minister*, pp. 138–139.

32. Heineman, *Hitler's First Foreign Minister*, pp. 140–141. Heineman cited as evidence, BA BL, R60964. Neurath to Hoesch, 23 March 1936.

33. For more on the Jewish question, see Christopher R. Browning, *The Final Solution and the German Foreign Office* (New York: Holmes & Meier, 1978), ch. 2 on *Referat Deutschland*. The controversial thesis recently advanced by Daniel Goldhagen, that Germans were uniquely anti-Semitic, possessed of an "eliminationist" mentality and merely awaiting the opportunity to act on their murderous convictions, finds no support from this study of the Foreign Ministry. While Neurath and his peers did not vigorously defend the Jews among their ranks, no evidence indicate that they either wished for or encouraged their extermination. See Daniel J. Goldhagen, *Hitler's Willing Executioners* (New York: Knopf, 1996).

34. Ernst von Weizsäcker, *Memoirs* (London: Victor Gollancz Ltd., 1951), p. 106.

35. Christian Leitz, *Economic Relations Between Nazi Germany and Franco's Spain, 1936–1945* (Oxford: Clarendon Press, 1996), pp. 15–16.

36. Weizsäcker, *Memoirs*, pp. 106–107.

37. Leitz, *Economic Relations*, p. 11.

38. Leitz, *Economic Relations*, p. 15.

39. Heineman, *Hitler's First Foreign Minister*, p. 151.

40. Weizsäcker, *Memoirs*, p. 109.

41. For an analysis of the Hoßbach memorandum, see Jonathan Wright and P. Stafford, "Hitler, Britain, and the Hoßbach Memorandum," *Militärgeschichtliche Mitteilungen* (vol. XLII, 1987).

42. Papen, *Memoirs*, p. 406.

43. Jürgen Gehl, *Austria, Germany, and the Anschluss* (London: Oxford University Press, 1963), p. 176, and Papen, *Memoirs*, pp. 406−407.

Betting It All

1. Johnson, *Nazi Terror*, p. 118.

2. Adolf Hitler, *Mein Kampf*, vol. 2 (New York: Reynal & Hitchcock, 1939), p. 965. This edition was published by arrangement with Houghton Mifflin Co., Boston.

3. David Dilks, *The Diaries of Sir Alexander Cadogan, O M, 193845* (London: Cassell and Co., 1971), pp. 87−88 (hereafter referred to as Cadogan, *Diaries*). Entries for July 16, 17, and 18, 1938.

4. Herbert von Dirksen, *Moskau-Tokio-London* (Stuttgart: W. Kohlhammer, 1949), pp. 215−217 Dirksen explained that Ribbentrop was to be kept as much in the dark as possible about these meetings. Dirksen also commented that Ribbentrop never forgave Wiedemann for this.

5. John Charmley, *Chamberlain and the Lost Peace* (London: Hodder & Stoughton, 1989), p. 164.

6. Andrew Roberts, *The Holy Fox: A Biography of Lord Halifax* (London: Weidenfeld and Nicolson, 1991), p. 161.

7. Roberts, *Holy Fox*, p. 162.

8. Donald C. Watt, *How War Came* (London: Mandarin, 1990), p. 25.

9. Martin Gilbert, who thoroughly researched the roots of appeasement, wrote of Wilson, who was given a room in 10 Downing Street when Chamberlain was prime minister: "He supported, encouraged, and perhaps initiated Chamberlain's foreign policy." Martin Gilbert and Richard Gott, *The Appeasers* (London: Weidenfeld & Nicholson, 1963), p. 359.

10. Helmut Metzmacher, "Deutsch-Englisch Ausgleichsbemühungen im Sommer 1939," *Vierteljahreshefte für Zeitgeschichte* (1966), p. 374.

11. Metzmacher, "Deutsch-Englisch," p. 374. In a private correspondence with Metzmacher in 1962, Wohlthat apparently admitted that he himself took the initiative in seeking a German-British rapprochement.

12. Watt, *How War Came*, p. 393.

13. A shortened version of Trott zu Solz's report eventually did reach Hitler through Walter Hewel. See Watt, *How War Came*, p. 393.

14. Sidney Aster, *1939: The Making of the Second World War* (London: Trinity Press, 1973), p. 245.

15. Hudson was critical of Chamberlain. On June 30, he wrote a private letter to Churchill expressing his doubts that Britain could convince Hitler of

British willingness to fight. He asked Churchill to "cut the Gordian knot" and form a war cabinet with Halifax. See Martin Gilbert, *Winston S. Churchill*, vol. V, companion part 3, *Documents: The Coming of War, 1936–1939* (London: Heinemann, 1982), pp. 1538–1540.

16. For an analysis of British "obsessive" fear of aerial bombardment, see Uri Bialer, *The Shadow of the Bomber: The Fear of Air Attack and British Politics* (London: Royal Historical Society, 1980), p. 151.

17. BA BL, Nachlaß Dirksen, 90 DI 1, Band 58/63-68. (Hereafter in this chapter Nachlaß Dirksen refers to the papers in the Bundesarchiv Berlin Lichterfelde.)

18. Nachlaß Dirksen, 90 Di 1, Band 58/63-68. Dirksen to Kordt, 21 July 1939.

19. Aster, *1939*, pp. 147–148. Wohlthat's files in the Public Record Office are closed until 2015. This may be because he had given sensitive information to Sir Robert Vansittart, or it may be because his files would be compromising for those involved.

20. Gilbert, *The Appeasers*, p. 226. Gilbert concluded that the July 21 meeting between Wilson and Wohlthat never occurred. However, Gilbert based this belief on Wilson's testimony in 1951 and the record Wilson made in his appointment book. "Wohlthat muddles his accounts of the various meetings that took place. He may well have thought that Wilson's name carried more weight at Berlin than Hudson's and tried to give the impression that Wilson had been his chief contact so that Berlin would take the plans more seriously." Gilbert also noted what W. J. Brown wrote of Wilson: "His influence was almost wholly bad. . . . In all the critical years, when swift, bold, strong action alone could have served our need, Wilson's temporizing, formula-evolving mind reinforced and emphasized the weakness of the Prime Minister" (p. 359).

21. Watt, *How War Came*, p. 400; and Aster, *1939*, p. 247.

22. For an interesting account of how a priest, a colonel, and a banker sought to maneuver the United States and Japan into peace before Pearl Harbor, see Robert Butow, *The John Doe Associates: Backdoor Diplomacy for Peace, 1941* (Stanford, CA: Stanford University Press, 1974).

23. Historians such as D. C. Watt, Gerhard Weinberg, and Sidney Aster have insisted that Buxton was acting solely on his own initiative. "Like Robert Hudson, Buxton was playing a lonely and dangerous hand." Aster, *1939*, p. 252.

24. Nachlaß Dirksen, Band 58/119-123.

25. See Hansard Parliamentary Debates, *House of Commons Official Report*, 5th series, vol. 350 (hereafter 350 HC DEB. 5S), p. 2023. The prime minister was attempting to defend the slow pace at which the triple alliance talks had been proceeding. He argued that treaties typically take months to negotiate and in this context referred to the 1904 and 1907 agreements. He also placed the blame for the slowness on the Soviets. "They preferred to sign nothing, to initial nothing, until we had got to a complete agreement, and as a result of that we were not able to present the world, as I would have liked to do, with even a provisional agree-

ment at an earlier stage." The evidence, including Cadogan's diaries, suggests the opposite, that it was Chamberlain who did not wish to sign an agreement with the Soviets.

26. Nachlaß Dirksen, 90 Di 1, Band 58/119-123.

27. Aster, *1939*, p. 254.

28. Nachlaß Dirksen, Band 58/96.

29. Nachlaß Dirksen, Band 58/100.

30. Nachlaß Dirksen, Band 58/97-99.

31. It is unlikely that the Foreign Office had any knowledge of the details surrounding Sir Horace's talks with either Wohlthat or Dirksen. There is no mention of them in Cadogan's diaries from June through mid-August. See Cadogan, *Diaries*, especially the editor's note on p. 192.

32. Charmley, *Chamberlain*, p. 194.

33. Aster, *1939*, pp. 256-257.

34. Nachlaß Dirksen, 90 Di 1, Band 58/139-148.

35. Nachlaß Dirksen, 90 Di 1, Band 58/139-148.

36. Nachlaß Dirksen, 90 Di 1. Band 58/149-154.

37. Watt asserted that Göring visited Hitler three times to press him to take up the British overtures that Wohlthat had related. This assertion, however, is based solely on an assumption. We cannot know what Göring said to Hitler in his private conversations. Watt's claim itself was based on Helmut Metzmacher's investigation of the Anglo-German talks, yet Metzmacher himself said that we can only guess at Göring's presentations to Hitler. Metzmacher concluded that it is impossible to know whether Hitler ever even saw Wohlthat's report. Metzmacher, "Deutsch-English," p. 400.

38. Nachlaß Dirksen, 90 Di 1, Band 58/184.

39. Nachlaß Dirksen, 90 Di 1, Band 58/184.

40. Nachlaß Dirksen, 90 Di 1, Band 58/185.

41. Nachlaß Dirksen, 90 Di 1, Band 58/185.

42. Dirksen, *Moskau*, pp. 243-259.

43. Dirksen, *Moskau*, p. 201.

44. Dirksen, *Moskau*, pp. 256-257.

45. Wolfgang Michalka, *Ribbentrop und die Deutsche Weltpolitik, 1933-40* (Munich: Wilhelm Fink Verlag, 1980), p. 250.

46. Metzmacher, "Deutsch-Englisch," p. 404.

47. Aster, *1939*, pp. 345-346. Cited in John Harvey, ed., *The Diplomatic Diaries of Oliver Harvey, 1937-1940* (1970), pp. 307-308.

48. Cadogan, *Diaries*, p. 203.

49. Ian Kershaw, *Hitler, 1936-1945: Nemesis* (New York:), p. 223, fn. 296.

Hitler's Trump Card

1. The month printed on this document is barely legible but appears to be September.

2. Gustav Hilger, *Wir und Der Kreml: Deutsch-Sowjetische Beziehungen 1918–1941, Erinnerungen eines deutschen Diplomaten* (Frankfurt am Main: Alfred Metzner, 1956), p. 267.

3. See Geoffrey Roberts, *The Soviet Union and the Origins of the Second World War: Russo-German Relations and the Road to War, 1933–1941* (London:), pp. 21–22. Cited in E. Gnedin, *Iz Istorii Otnoshenii Mezhdu SSSR i Fashistskoi Germaniei* (New York: 1977), pp. 34–35.

4. Although barely legible, the symbols "31 M" appear atop the document. Based on additional information contained within the report and that drawn from others in the collection, the date is presumably March 31, 1937. This same information regarding Hitler's worries over shortages in raw materials and his desire to maintain neutral relations with Russia was reiterated in an undated second document.

5. Unless stated otherwise, citations concerning Schulenburg are drawn from the NKVD files on the German ambassador, now located in the Bundesarchiv Koblenz, Kleine Erwerbung Nr. 903. Intelligence reports must be read with considerable caution. It is impossible to determine the identities of the agents who obtained this information; nor can we know whether personal agendas may have motivated them to exaggerate their data in hope of gaining their superiors' attention. Following the purges in the mid-1930s, an atmosphere of fear and uncertainty surely affected some NKVD agents, especially since the two intelligence chiefs who preceded Beria were executed. Despite these drawbacks, the files offer fresh perspectives on Nazi-Soviet relations in the inter-war period and are worth considering.

6. Only Geoffrey Roberts has contended that Litvinov was not in favor of an alliance with the Western democracies but instead desired alignment with Hitler.Geoffrey Roberts, "The Alliance That Failed: Moscow and the Triple Alliance Negotiations, 1939," *European History Quarterly* (July 1996), 26:3.

7. Paul R. Sweet, ed., *Documents on German Foreign Policy, 1918–1945,* Series D, vol. I (Washington, DC: Government Printing Office, 1956), pp. 920–921.

8. Sweet, *Documents,*, pp. 928–929.

9. David Irving, *The War Path: Hitler's Germany, 1933–1939* (London: Macmillan, 1978), pp. 241–242. Irving wrote: "Admiral Boehm, the fleet commander, quoted Hitler in his note as saying: 'That same evening the Ambassador expressed his thanks to me for this and for not having given him the second-class treatment at the reception.'"

10. Citation of Brammer's notes are from BA K, Zsg. 101, Nachlaß Brammer.

11. Ingeborg Fleischhauer, *Der Pakt: Hitler, Stalin und die Initiative der deutschen Diplomatie* (Berlin: Ullstein, 1990), p. 411.

12. See *Nazi-Soviet Relations*, pp. 1–2.

13. *God Krizisa, 1938–1939. Dokumenty i Materialy,* 2 vols. (Moscow, 1990), vol. 1, doc. 279, p. 389. 18 April 1939. Merekalov to Litvinov.

14. Roberts, *The Soviet Union*, p. 71.

15. *God Krizisa*, vol. 1, doc. 252, p. 360. 5 April 1939. Litvinov to Merekalov.

16. *God Krizisa*, vol. 1, doc. 276, pp. 386–387. Litvinov to Seeds. 17 April 1939. See also Aleksandr M. Nekrich, *Pariahs, Partners, Predators: German-Soviet Relations, 1922–1941* (New York: Columbia Univ. Press, 1977), p. 104.

17. Bullock, *Hitler and Stalin*, p. 651.

18. Bullock, *Hitler and Stalin*, p. 651. See also Hermann Teske, ed., *General Ernst Köstring: Der Militärische Mittler Zwischen dem Deutschen Reich und der Sowjetunion, 1921–1941* (Frankfurt am Main: Verlag Mittler und Sohn, 1965), p. 134

19. Teske, *General Ernst Köstring*, pp. 135–137.

20. PA, R 29712/1/23-24. Büro des Staatssekretärs, Akten Betreffend Rußland.

21. As noted in the introduction, the final judgment on Weizsäcker cannot be made until all the relevant documents are released. Until the documents for this period, currently held in the family archives, are made available, Weizsäcker's true role in the Nazi-Soviet pact must remain unknown.

22. *ADAP*, D, VI/490-93. Ribbentrop's own words were, "Gewisse Anzeigen für die sowjetrussische Auffassung in dieser Richtung haben wir in der Rede Stalins im März zu erkennen geglaubt."

23. Weizsäcker, *Memoirs*, p. 190.

24. Kordt, *Nicht aus den Akten*, p. 310.

25. Kordt, *Nicht aus den Akten,*, p. 315, and Weizsäcker, *Memoirs*, p. 190.

26. Hans-Heinrich Herwarth von Bittenfeld, *Against Two Evils: Memoirs of a Diplomat-Soldier During the Third Reich* (London: Collins, 1981), pp. 148–167. Admiral Canaris, head of the German Intelligence Service, was also leaking information to the Italian military attaché in Berlin regarding the secret Moscow-Berlin talks.

27. Schulenburg was later hanged for his participation in the July plot to assassinate Hitler.

28. Charles E. Bohlen, *Witness to History, 1929–1969* (London: Weidenfeld & Nicolson, 1973), pp. 69–89.

29. Watt, *How War Came*, pp. 245–246.

30. Cadogan, *Diaries*, p. 182, and Roberts, *Holy Fox*, p. 158.

31. Watt, *How War Came*, p. 246.

32. Hansard Parliamentary Debates, *House of Commons Official Report*, 5th series, vol. 350 (hereafter 350 HC DEB. 5S), p. 1929.

33. *DGFP*, D/VI, pp. 1006–1009.

34. Aster, *1939*, p. 299.

35. Herwarth, *Against Two Evils*, p. 167.

36. Watt, *How War Came*, pp. 116, 231, 248.

37. Dmitri Volkogonov, *Stalin: Triumph and Tragedy* (London: 1991), p. 353.

38. PA, Botschaft Moskau, 515, Politische Beziehungen Deutschland zu England, "Einkreisungspolitik." Copy of report from Dirksen to AA. 24 July 1939. Arrived in Moscow Embassy on August 3, read by Schulenburg on August 11.

Conclusions

1. Adolf Hitler's remark to General Franz Halder upon appointing him army chief of staff. Bullock, *Hitler and Stalin*, p. 621. Cited Gen. Franz Halder, *Tagebücher*, August 2, 1938.

Bibliography

Because the literature on Nazi Germany is so extensive, only those works of particular value for this work are cited.

Unpublished Sources

Below are listed only those larger collections of documents from which valuable information was drawn. The many other files, such as those involving political relations between Germany and other nations, especially those housed in the Foreign Ministry archives, have been cited in the notes.

Bundesarchiv Berlin Lichterfelde:

1. Handakten, Foreign Minister Constantin Freiherr von Neurath
2. Nachlaß, Ambassador Herbert von Dirksen
3. Nachlaß, Embassy Advisor Gustav Hilger
4. Nachlaß, Ambassador Friedrich Werner Graf von der Schulenburg
5. Nachlaß, Ambassador Oskar von Traumann

Politisches Archiv des Auswärtigen Amts, Bonn:

1. Handakten, State Secretary Bernhard Wilhelm von Bülow
2. Nachlaß, Ministry official Gottfried Aschmann
3. Nachlaß, Ministry official Lieres von Wilkau
4. Berichte und Aufzeichnungen der Militärattachés, London, Paris, Warsaw

Bundesarchiv Koblenz:

1. Nachlaß, Foreign Minister Constantin Freiherr von Neurath
2. Handakten and Personal Papers, State Secretary Ernst von Weizsäcker
3. Zsg. 101, Notes of journalist Karl Brammer
4. NKVD Files on Ambassador Schulenburg, Kleine Erwerbung Nr. 903

Published Sources

Domarus, Max. *Hitler, Reden und Proklamation, 1932–1945*, Wiesbaden, 1973.
Dokumenty Vneshnei Politiki, vol. 22, books 1–2, Moscow, 1992.
God Krizisa, 1938–1939. Dokumenty i Materialy, 2 vols., Moscow, 1990.
Hansard Parliamentary Debates, *House of Commons Official Report*, 5th series, vol. 350.
Hill, Leonidas E., ed. *Die Weizsäcker-Papiere, 1933–1950*. Berlin, 1974.
Hitler, Adolf. *Mein Kampf*. New York, Reynal & Hitchcock, 1939. Published by arrangement with Houghton Mifflin Co., Boston, Mass.
Hitler, Adolf. *Hitlers Zweites Buch*. New York, 1962.
Hitler, Adolf. *The Testament of Adolf Hitler: The Hitler-Bormann Documents, February–April 1945*. London, 1960.
Sontag, Raymond J., and James Stuart Beddie. *Nazi-Soviet Relations, 1939–1941: Documents from the Archives of the German Foreign Office*. Washington, 1948.
Sweet, Paul R. *Documents on German Foreign Policy, 1918–45*, Series C and D. Washington, DC, 1956.
Trial of the Major War Criminals before the International Military Tribunal: Proceedings, vols. 1–22. Nuremberg, 1947–1949.
Polish Ministry for Foreign Affairs, Polish White Book, Official Documents Concerning Polish-German and Polish-Soviet Relations, 1933–1939. New York.

Diaries and Memoirs

Bohlen, Charles E. *Witness to History, 1929–1969*. London, 1973.
Cadogan, Sir Alexander. *The Diaries of Sir Alexander Cadogan, O M, 1938–1945*. London, 1971, David Dilks (ed.).
Dirksen, Herbert von. *Moskau-Tokio-London*. Stuttgart, 1949.
Dodd, William E. *Ambassador Dodd's Diary*. New York, 1941.
François-Poncet, André. *The Fateful Years: Memoirs of a French Ambassador in Berlin, 1931–1938*. New York, 1949.
Fromm, Bella. *Blood and Banquets: A Berlin Social Diary*. London, 1942.
Goebbels, Joseph. *Die Tagebücher von Joseph Goebbels: Teil I, Aufzeichnungen, 1924–1941*, Munich, 1987, Elke Frölich (ed.).
Hägglof, Gunnar. *Diplomat: Memoirs of a Swedish Envoy*. London, 1972.
Harvey, Oliver. *The Diplomatic Diaries of Oliver Harvey, 1937–1940*. 1970, John Harvey, ed.

Herwarth, Hans-Heinrich von Bittenfeld. *Against Two Evils: Memoirs of a Diplo-mat-Soldier During the Third Reich.* London, 1981.

Hilger, Gustav. *Wir und der Kreml: Deutsch-Sowjetische Beziehungen 1918–1941, Erinnerungen eines deutschen Diplomaten.* Frankfurt am Main, 1956.

Hoßbach, Friedrich. *Zwischen Wehrmacht und Hitler, 1934–1938.* Wolffen-büttel, 1949.

Kirkpatrick, Ivone. *The Inner Circle: Memoirs of Ivone Kirkpatrick.* London, 1959.

Klemperer, Viktor. *I Will Bear Witness: A Diary of the Nazi Years, 1933–1941.* New York, 1998.

Kordt, Erich. *Nicht aus den Akten . . . Die Wilhelmstraße in Frieden und Krieg, Erlebnisse, Begegnungen, und Eindrücke, 1928–1945.* Stuttgart, 1950.

Köstring, Ernst. *General Ernst Köstring: Der Militärische Mittler zwischen dem Deutschen Reich und der Sowjetunion, 1921–1941.* Frankfurt a.M., 1965.

Krogmann, Karl Vincent. *Es Ging um Deutschlands Zukunft, 1932–1939.* Lands-berg am Lech, 1976.

Krosigk, Lutz Graf Schwerin von. *Es Geschah in Deutschland: Menschenbilder unseres Jahrhunderts.* Tübingen, 1951.

Nadolny, Rudolf. *Mein Beitrag: Erinnerungen eines Botschafters des Dritten Reiches.* Cologne, 1985.

Papen, Franz von. *Memoirs.* London, 1952.

Raeder, Erich. *Struggle for the Sea.* London, 1959.

Schacht, Hjalmar. *Abrechnung mit Hitler.* London, 1949.

Schmidt, Dr. Paul. *Statist auf diplomatischer Bühne, 1923–1945: Erlebnisse des Chefdolmetschers im Auswärtgen Amt mit den Staatsmännern Europas.* Bonn, 1949.

Speer, Albert. *Inside the Third Reich.* New York, 1970.

Wheeler-Bennett, Sir John. *Knaves, Fools, and Heroes: Europe Between the Wars.* London, 1974.

Weizsäcker, Ernst von. *Memoirs.* London, 1951.

Secondary Works

Adamthwaite, Anthony. *France and the Coming of the Second World War 1936–39.* London, 1977.

Allen, William Sheridan. *The Nazi Seizure of Power.* New York, 1984.

Allison, Graham. *Essence of Decision: Explaining the Cuban Missile Crisis.* Boston, 1971.

Aster, Sidney. *1939: The Making of the Second World War.* London, 1973.

Axelrod, Robert. *The Evolution of Co-operation.* London, 1990.

Bear, George W. *Test Case: Italy, Ethiopia, and the League of Nations.* Stan-ford, 1976.

Beloff, Max. *The Foreign Policy of Soviet Russia, 1929–1941.* London, 1949.

Bennett, Edward W. *German Rearmament and the West, 1932–1933.* Prince-ton, 1979.

Beradt, Charlotte. *Third Reich of Dreams*. Northhamptonshire, 1985.

Bialer, Uri. *The Shadow of the Bomber: The Fear of Air Attack and British Politics*. London, 1980.

Bloch, Michael. *Ribbentrop*. New York, 1992.

Bracher, Karl Dietrich, Manfred Funke, and Hans-Adolf Jacobsen. *Die Weimarer Republik, 1918–1933*. Düsseldorf, 1987.

———. *Deutschland 1933–1945: Neue Studien zur Nationalsozialistischen Herrschaft.*, Düsseldorf, 1992.

Bracher, Karl Dietrich. *The German Dictatorship*. Harmondsworth, 1973.

Braubach, Max. *Der Einmarsch deutscher Truppen in die entmilitarisierte Zone am Rhein in März 1936: Ein Beitrag zur Vorgeschichte des Zweiten Weltkrieges*. Cologne, 1956.

Broszat, Martin. *Nationalsozialistische Polenpolitik, 1939–1945*. Stuttgart, 1961.

Browning, Christopher R. *The Final Solution and the German Foreign Office*. New York, 1978.

Brysac, Shareen Blair. *Resisting Hitler: Mildred Harnack and the Red Orchestra*. Oxford, 2000.

Bullock, Alan. *Hitler: A Study in Tyranny*. Harmondsworth, 1962.

———. *Hitler and Stalin: Parallel Lives*. New York, 1991.

Burleigh, Michael. *The Third Reich: A New History*. New York, 2000.

Butow, Robert. *The John Doe Associates: Backdoor Diplomacy for Peace, 1941*. Stanford, CA, 1974.

Carr, E. H. *German-Soviet Relations Between the Two World Wars*.

Carley, Michael. *1939: The Alliance That Never Was and the Coming of World War Two*. Chicago, 1999.

Carsten, F. L. *Reichswehr und Politik, 1919–1933*. Köln, 1964.

Cecil, Robert. *The Myth of the Master Race: Alfred Rosenberg and Nazi Ideology*. Birkenhead, 1972.

Charmley, John. *Chamberlain and the Lost Peace*. London, 1989.

Childers, Thomas. *The Nazi Voter: Social Foundations of Fascism in Germany, 1919–1933*. London, 1983.

Davies, Norman. *God's Playground: A History of Poland in Two Volumes*. Oxford, 1981.

Dahrendorf, Ralf. *Society and Democracy in Germany*. London, 1968.

Deakin, F. W., and Richard Storry. *The Case of Richard Sorge*. London, 1966.

Deist, Wilhelm (ed.). *Das Deutsche Reich und der Zweite Weltkrieg: Ursachen und Voraussetzungen der Deutschen Kriegspolitik*. Stuttgart, 1979.

———. *The Wehrmacht and German Rearmament*. London, 1981.

———. *The Build-up of German Aggression*. Oxford, 1990.

Doenitz, Karl. *Ten Years and 20 Days*. London, 1959.

Dulffer, Jost. *Weimar, Hitler, und die Marine: Reichspolitik und Flottenbau, 1920–1939*. Düsseldorf, 1973.

Emmerson, Thomas James. *The Rhineland Crisis, 7 March 1936: A Study in Multilateral Diplomacy*. London, 1977.

Fest, Joachim C. *Hitler.* London, 1974.

Finkel, Alvin, and Clement Leibovitz. *The Chamberlain-Hitler Collusion.* Suffolk, 1997.

Fleischhauer, Ingeborg. *Der Pakt: Hitler, Stalin und die Initiative der deutschen Diplomatie.* Berlin, 1990.

Freund, Gerald. *Unholy Alliance: Russian-German Relations from the Treaty of Brest-Litovsk to the Treaty of Berlin.* London, 1957.

Funke, Manfred. "7. *März 1936. Fallstudie zum außenpolitischen Führungsstil Hitlers,*" in Wolfgang Michalka (ed.), *Nationalsozialistische Außenpolitik.* Darmstadt, 1978, 277–324.

Gallo, Max. *The Night of the Long Knives.* London, 1972.

Gatzke, Hans. *Stresemann and the Rearmament of Germany.* Baltimore, 1954.

Gehl, Jürgen. *Austria, Germany, and the Anschluss.* London, 1963.

Gellately, Robert. *The Gestapo and German Society: Enforcing Racial Policy, 1933–1945.* Oxford, 1990.

———. *Backing Hitler: Consent and Coercion in Nazi Germany.* Oxford, 2001.

George, Alexander L. *Presidential Decision-Making in Foreign Policy: The Effective Use of Information and Advice.* Boulder, 1980.

———. *Bridging the Gap: Theory and Practice in Foreign Policy.* Washington, 1993.

Geyer, Michael. *Aufrüstung oder Sicherheit: Die Reichswehr in der Krise der Machtpolitik 1924–1936.* Wiesbaden, 1980.

Gilbert, Martin. *Winston S. Churchill,* vol. 5, companion part 3, *Documents: The Coming of War, 1936–1939.* London, 1982.

Gilbert, Martin, and Richard Gott. *The Appeasers.* London, 1967.

Gill, Anton. *An Honourable Defeat: The Fight Against National Socialism in Germany, 1933–1945.* London, 1994.

Gnedin, E. *Iz Istorii Otnoshenii Mezhdu SSSR: Fashistskoi Germaniei.* New York, 1977.

Goldhagen, Daniel J. *Hitler's Willing Executioners.* Berlin, 1996.

Gorodetsky, Gabriel (ed.). *Soviet Foreign Policy, 1917–1991: A Retrospective.* London, 1994.

———. *Grand Delusion: Stalin and the German Invasion of Russia.* New Haven, 1999.

Haftendorn, Helga. "Zur Theorie außenpolitischer Entscheidungsprozesse," in Volker Rittberger, *Theorien der Internationalen Beziehungen: Bestandsaufnahme und Forschungsperspektiven.* Opladen, 1990.

Handel, Michael. *Masters of War: Classical Strategic Thought.* London, 1996.

———. *The Diplomacy of Surprise: Hitler, Nixon, Sadat.* Cambridge, MA, 1981.

Gathorne-Hardy, G. M. *A Short History of International Affairs, 1920–1939.* London, 1950.

Heineman, John L. *Hitler's First Foreign Minister: Constantin Freiherr von Neurath, Diplomat and Statesman.* Berkeley, 1979.

Herwig, Holger. *Politics of Frustration: The United States in German Naval Planning, 1889–1941*. Boston, 1976.

Hildebrand, Klaus. *Das Vergangene Reich: Deutsche Außenpolitik von Bismarck bis Hitler, 1871–1945*. Stuttgart, 1995.

———. *Vom Reich zum Weltreich: Hitler, NSDAP, und die koloniale Frage*. Munich, 1969.

Hillgruber, Andreas. *Hitlers Strategie: Politik und Kriegfuhrung, 1940–1941*. Munich, 1982.

———. *Kontinuitat und Diskontinuitatin der deutschen Aussenpolitik von Bismarck bis Hitler*. Dusseldorf, 1969.

Hogan, Michael, and Thomas Patterson. *Explaining the History of American Foreign Relations*. Cambridge, 1991.

Höhne, Heinz. *Die Zeit der Illlusionen, Hitler un die Anfänge des 3. Reiches 1933 bis 1936*. Düsseldorf, 1991.

Iklé, Frank. *German-Japanese Relations, 1936–1940*. New York, 1956.

Iriye, Akira. *After Imperialism: The Search for a New Order in the Far East, 1921–1931*. New York, 1969.

Irving, David. *Breach of Security: The German Secret Intelligence File on Events Leading to the Second World War*. London, 1968.

———. *The War Path: Hitler's Germany, 1933–1939*, London, 1978.

Jacobsen, Hans-Adolf. *Nationalsozialistische Außenpolitik, 1933–1938*. Frankfurt a.M., 1968.

Jäckel, Eberhard. *Hitler's World View*. Cambridge, MA, 1981.

James, Harold. *The German Slump: Politics and Economics, 1924–1936*. Oxford, 1986.

James, Robet Rhodes. *Chips: The Diaries of Sir Henry Channon*. London, 1967.

Janis, Irving L., and Leon Mann. *Decision Making: A Psychological Analysis of Conflict, Choice, and Commitment*. New York, 1977.

Jervis, Robert. *Perception and Misperception in International Politics*. Princeton, 1976.

Johnson, Eric A. *Nazi Terror: The Gestapo, Jews, and Ordinary Germans*. New York, 1999.

Kahn, David. *Hitler's Spies: German Military Intelligence in World War II*. New York, 1978.

Kaiser, David E. *Economic Diplomacy and the Origins of the Second World War: Germany, Britain, France, and Eastern Europe, 1930–1939*. Princeton, 1980.

Kershaw, Ian. *The Nazi Dictatorship: Problems and Perspectives*. Hamburg, 1988.

———. *The Hitler Myth: Image and Reality in the Third Reich*. Oxford, 1987.

———. (ed.). *Weimar: Why Did German Democracy Fail*. London, 1990.

———.and Moshe Lewin (eds.). *Stalinism and Nazism: Dictatorships in Comparison*. Cambridge, UK, 1997.

———. *Hitler, 1889–1936: Hubris*. London, 1998.

———. *Hitler: Nemesis, 1936–1945*. New York, 1999.

Kimmich, Christoph. *German Foreign Policy 1918–45: A Guide to Research and Research Materials*. Wilmington, 1991.

———. *The Free City: Danzig and German Foreign Policy, 1919–1934*. New Haven, 1968.

Klemperer, Klemens von. *German Resistance against Hitler: The Search for Allies Abroad, 1938–1945*. Oxford, 1992.

Kolasky, John. *Partners in Tyranny: The Nazi Soviet Non-Aggression Pact, 1939*. Toronto, 1990.

Krüger, Peter, and Erich Hahn. "Loyalitätskonflikt des Staatsekretärs Bernhard Wilhelm von Bülow im Frühjahr 1933." *VfZ*, 4, 376–410.

Krüger, Peter. *Die Außenpolitik der Republik von Weimar*. Darmstadt, 1985.

Kube, Alfred. *Pour le Mérité und Hackenkreuz: Hermann Göring im Dritten Reich*. Munich, 1986.

Leitz, Christian. *Economic Relations Between Nazi Germany and Franco's Spain, 1936–1945*. Oxford, 1996.

Lipski, Jozef. *Diplomat in Berlin, 1933–1939*. New York, 1968.

Mack Smith, Dennis. *Mussolini's Roman Empire*. New York, 1977.

Martin, Bernd. *Formierung und Fall der Achse Berlin-Tokio*. Munich, 1994.

———. *Japan and Germany in the Modern World*. Oxford, 1995.

Mau, Hermann. "Die 'Zweite Revolution' – der 30. Juni 1934." *VfZ*, 1 (1953), 119–137.

May, Ernest R. *"Lessons" of the Past: The Use and Misuse of History in American Foreign Policy*. New York, 1973.

McMurry, Dean Scott. *Deutschland und die Sowjetunion, 1933–1936: Ideologie, Machtpolitik, und Wirtschaftsbeziehungen*. Cologne, 1979.

Menzel Meskill, Johanna. *Hitler and Japan: The Hollow Alliance*. New York, 1966.

Metzmacher, Helmut. "Deutsch-Englisch Ausgleichsbemühungen im Sommer 1939." *VfZ* (1966).

Michalka, Wolfgang. *Ribbentrop und die Deutsche Weltpolitik, 1933–1940*. Munich, 1980.

Mommsen, Hans. *Beamtentum im Dritten Reich*. Stuttgart, 1966.

———. *From Weimar to Auschwitz*. Princeton, 1991.

Müller, Klaus-Jergen. *General Ludwig Beck: Studien und Dokumente zur politisch-militärisch Vorstellungswelt und Tätigkeit des Generalstabschefs des deutschen Heeres, 1933–1938*. Boppard am Rhein, 1980.

Naumann, Friedrich. *Central Europe*. New York, 1917.

Nekrich, Aleksandr M. *Pariahs, Partners, Predators: German-Soviet Relations, 1922–1941*. New York: Columbia University Press, 1997.

Nicholls, Anthony. The Bavarian Background to National Socialism," in Anthony Nicholls and Erich Matthias (eds.), *German Democracy and the Triumph of Hitler*. London, 1971, 99–128.

Nicholls, Anthony. *Weimar and the Rise of Hitler*. London, 1991.

Niedhart, Gottfried. *Kriegsbeginn 1939: Entfesselung oder Ausbruch des Zweiten Weltkriegs.* Darmstadt, 1976.

Nish, Ian. *Japanese Foreign Policy, 1869–1942.* London, 1977.

Noakes, Jeremy, and G. Pridham (eds.). *A Documentary Reader: Nazism, 1919–1945,* 4 vols. Exeter, 1983.

O'Neill, Robert. *The German Army and the Nazi Party, 1933–1939.* London, 1966.

Orlow, Dietrich. *The History of the Nazi Party, 1933–1945.* Pittsburgh, 1973.

Parker, R. A. C. *Chamberlain and Appeasement: British Policy and the Coming of the Second World War.* London, 1993.

Peterson, Edward N. *The Limits of Hitler's Power.* Princeton, 1969.

Post, Gaines. *The Civil-Military Fabric of Weimar Foreign Policy.* Princeton, 1973.

———. *Dilemmas of Appeasement: British Deterrence and Defense 1934–1937.* Ithaca, 1993.

Rahn, Werner. *Reichsmarine und Landesverteidigung, 1919–1928.* Munich, 1976.

Rauch, Georg von. "Der Deutsch-Sovjetische Nichtangriffspakt vom August 1939 und die Sovjetische Geschichtsforschung," in Niedhart, *Kriegsbeginn,* 349–366.

Rauschning, Hermann. *Gespräche mit Hitler.* Vienna, 1973.

Reynolds, Nicholas. *Treason Was No Crime: Ludwig Beck, Chief of the German General Staff.* London, 1976.

Roberts, Andrew. *The Holy Fox: A Biography of Lord Halifax.* London, 1991.

Roberts, Geoffrey. "The Alliance That Failed: Moscow and the Triple Alliance Negotiations." *European History Quarterly* (1996), 26, 3–.

———. *The Unholy Alliance: Stalin's Pact with Hitler.* London, 1989.

———. *The Soviet Union and the Origins of the Second World War: Russo-German Relations and the Road to War, 1933–1941.* London, 1995.

Roos, Hans. *A History of Modern Poland.* London, 1966.

Salewski, Michael. "Die Verteidigung der Ostsee, 1918–1939: Politische und Strategische Konzeption," in *Marine Rundschau,* 69, 1972, 385–401.

———. "Zur Deutschen Sicherheitspolitik in der Spätzeit der Weimarer Republik." *VfZ,* (1974), 22, 121–147.

Schreiber, Gerhard. *Revisionismus und Weltmachtstreben.* Stuttgart, 1978.

———. Bernd Stegemann, and Detlef Vogel, (eds.). *Das Deutsche Reich und der Zweite Weltkrieg,* vol. 3. Stuttgart, 1984.

Schöllgen, Gregor. *A Conservative against Hitler: Ulrich von Hassell: Diplomat in Imperial Germany, The Weimar Republic, and the Third Reich, 1881–1944.* London, 1991.

Schuker, Stephen A. "France and the Remilitarization of the Rhineland, 1936." *French Historical Studies* (1986), 299–337.

Sereny, Gitta. *Albert Speer: His Battle With Truth.* London, 1996.

Smith, Dennis Mack. *Mussolini's Roman Empire.* London, 1976.

Sommer, Theo. *Deutschland und Japan Zwischen den Mächten, 1935–1940.* Tübingen, 1962.

Stachura, Peter D. *Gregor Strasser and the Rise of Nazism.* London, 1983.

Suvorov, Viktor. *Icebreaker: Who Started the Second World War?* London, 1990.

Taylor, A. J. P. *The Origins of the Second World War.* Harmondsworth, 1964.

Thies, Jochen. *Architekt der Weltherrschaft: Die "Endziele" Hitlers.* Düsseldorf, 1976.

Turner, Henry Ashby. *German Big Business and the Rise of Hitler.* Oxford, 1985.

Volkogonov, Dmitri. *Stalin: Triumph and Tragedy.* London, 1991.

Watt, Donald Cameron. *How War Came.* London, 1990.

Weinberg, Gerhard. *Germany and the Soviet Union, 1939–1941.* Leiden, 1–954.

———. *The Foreign Policy of Hitler's Germany: Diplomatic Revolution in Europe, 19331936.* Chicago, 1970.

———. *The Foreign Policy of Hitler's Germany: Starting World War II.* Chicago, 1980.

———. *Germany, Hitler, and World War Two.* Cambridge, 1995.

Whealey, Robert H. *Hitler and Spain: The Nazi Role in the Spanish Civil War, 1936–1939.* Lexington, 1989.

Wheeler-Bennett, Sir John W. *The Nemesis of Power: The German Army in Politics, 1918–1945.* London, 1953.

Winkler, Heinrich August. *Weimar, 1918–1933: Die Geschichte der ersten deutschen Demokratie.* Munich, 1993.

Wollstein, Gunter. *Vom Weimarer Revisionismus zu Hitler.* Bonn, 1973.

Wright, Jonathan, and P. Stafford. "Hitler, Britain, and the Hossbach Memorandum," in *Militär-Geschichtliche Mitteilungen,* vol. 42, 1987.

Yang, Jennifer. *British Policy and Strategy in the Tientsen Crisis, 1939.* Unpublished M Litt. thesis, 1994, Oxford University.

Young, Robert J. *In Command of France: French Foreign Policy and Military Planning 1933–1940.* Cambridge, 1978.

Index